PATANJALI'S

how timeless yoga wisdom can

YOGA SUTRAS

revolutionize our lives today

Giridhari Das

PATANJALI'S

how timeless yoga wisdom can

YOGA SUTRAS

revolutionize our lives today

Patanjali's Yoga Sutras Revolution
1st Edition - © 2018 Giridhari Das.
All rights reserved. No part of this book may be reproduced in any form without permission from the publisher.
For more information about Patanjali's Yoga Sutras Revolution and Giridhari Das, please visit www.3tpath.com

ISBN: 978-85-69942-28-3

Illustrations: Bruna Lima (Bindu Mādhava Devi Dasi)
Illustrations on page 70: Pedro Luis (@pedroluiss)
Cover Designer: Mateus Dias (Narada Muni Dasa)
Editor: Carl Herzig and Thiago Costa Braga (Bhagavan Dasa)
Proofreader: Susan Seidenberg and Robson Silva da Silva
Layout editor: Jeferson Rocha

Table of contents

Preface 7
Introduction 9
Samadhi-pada 13
Sadhana-pada 69
Vibhuti-pada 105
Kaivalya-pada 127
Conclusion 145
About the author 149

Preface

Why bother reading a 2,000-year-old book about the mind and well-being? The world is changing so fast, and science is bringing us new discoveries on the workings of the brain, positive psychology, and the study of well-being. So why look back?

I would argue that we should look back because much of the cutting-edge information transforming people's lives today has its roots in the ancient science of yoga. Long before the time of Jesus, yogis recognized the human need for meaning, peace and clarity of mind, and transcendence; knew the value of focus; and studied and practiced mindfulness and meditation. Their teachings have guided practitioners for centuries and for more than thirty years have inspired research in the fields of positive psychology and neuroscience.

There are two core books in the yoga tradition: the *Yoga Sutras* of Patanjali and the *Bhagavad-gita*, spoken by Krishna. The *Yoga Sutras* is considered to be about 2,000 years old; the *Bhagavad-gita* is much older than that.

These two books, with *Srimad-Bhagavatam*, are what inspired me to dedicate my life to the path of self-improvement and self-realization in yoga. In my 2017 book, *The 3T Path*, I explain what yoga is and present the path in its entirety.

My purpose for this version of Patanjali's *Yoga Sutras* is to offer a simple, practical presentation of this ancient text. The *Yoga Sutras* can be hard to decipher, let alone put into practice, but I hope you'll find this book both useful and easy to understand. I've taken help from my spiritual master, Hridayananda Das Goswami, and the comprehensive work done on the *Yoga Sutras* by Edwin F. Bryant, and also drawn from my twenty-five years of experience living and teaching this great science of the mind and spirit.

This is my second *Yoga Sutras*. The first, published in 2006, was based on the translations and explanations given by my spiritual master. Now, with all that I've learned since, I feel that it is time for another version, sharing my own realizations. I especially want to share key aspects of my work that have proven effective in enhancing the quality of people's lives.

There is so much we can do to make our lives better and because it involves just you and your mind, there's equal opportunity for all of us. Everybody can learn and gradually apply the knowledge and techniques to do this in their lives. With less effort than you might imagine, you can get abundant results. This yoga tradition pinpoints both the cause of our suffering and the means to fix it.

The world is waking up to this knowledge. Science is studying it. Its life-changing concepts are being introduced in business, education, government, and all facets of private life. I hope this book will help you uncover and apply some of this remarkable knowledge.

Introduction

What is a sutra?

Sutra is a Sanskrit term meaning a thread, string, or line. It is also a genre of Vedic literature that presents knowledge in a condensed form. The *Yoga Sutras* are a concise presentation of yoga, according to the great sage Patanjali.

Due to their sometimes-cryptic nature, sutras are traditionally accompanied by commentaries that explain their meanings, and so almost every sutra in this book will be followed comments and explanations to help you develop your understanding of Patanjali's concepts and how they can help you live a better life.

The *Yoga Sutras* describe the essence of yoga—its practical elements, obstacles, intermediary results, and final goal.

How are the Yoga Sutras presented?

The *Yoga Sutras* are divided into four chapters, called *padas*, steps.

Samadhi-pada: The first step is about *samadhi*, the final state of enlightenment. Since *samadhi* is the final step, you might find it curious that it comes first in the book, but this is not uncommon in yoga texts. Krishna does something similar in the *Bhagavad-gita*—describes the highest state first. The subsequent text then helps the reader understand how that state is achieved and provides other useful information about the process. This chapter starts by first describing the basics of what consciousness is, then how perfection is achieved, and finally the ultimate, perfect state.

Sadhana-pada: The second step is about the practice necessary to achieve *samadhi—sadhana*. Picture this scene: A student is sitting in front of Patanjali, having just heard the first chapter, but he still doesn't understand how one is supposed to achieve *samadhi*. "My dear master," he asks, "could you kindly explain in more detail how one practices yoga to achieve *samadhi*?" Patanjali then describes the process in greater detail.

So, the first chapter contains the final state of yoga and this second chapter starts with the basics. A close examination will show that in this chapter, Patanjali, like Krishna in the *Bhagavad-gita*, describes two separate processes: one, more general and practical, that I call the Path of Enlightened Life, and the other, more specific, for those who wish to follow the path of meditation-only yoga.

Vibhuti-pada: The third step begins by delineating the final stages of meditation-only yoga and then describes the superpowers (*vibhutis*) one can achieve. Most of the chapter reads like a guide to gaining superpowers, explaining how each is gained as the yogi directs his or her high-level mental focus toward different objects or parts of the body.

Kaivalya-pada: The fourth and final step is again perfection, this time described by the word *kaivalya*, which can mean "perfect union" or "isolation." Since the word *yoga* means union and the object of yoga is to isolate consciousness from matter, both meanings are quite fitting. In this chapter, there are some key facts about the process of yoga and descriptions of what perfection in yoga is like.

All together, there are 196 sutras in the book: 51 in the first chapter, 55 in the second, 56 in the third, and 34 in the fourth.

How is this version presented?

Each sutra is accompanied by a simple but comprehensive translation. I have tried to find a balance between a literal translation, which can be more faithful to the Sanskrit but harder to read and understand, and a looser translation, which might be easier for the reader but can be more the author's words than Patanjali's. I tried to stay close to the original text but make it clear for the reader.

My goal here is to make the Yoga Sutras as practical as possible. The comments are meant to shed light on the original text and provide you with knowledge on two levels. The first level is simply understanding what the sutra means, expanding the meaning and explaining the concepts behind it. Second, whenever possible, I'll show you how you can put each sutra into practice to improve your life.

The aim here is to make reading the sutras a fun and useful experience. I want you to enjoy the reading and discover the many amazing ways this text can revolutionize your life.

The world needs a revolution of consciousness. We must change the way we go about life and how we deal with one another and with the environment. In this book, you'll see how yoga can provide us with the blueprint for this revolution.

Samadhi-pada

1. Now, instructions on yoga.

Though simple enough to understand, this first sutra has hidden meaning extrapolated from the Sanskrit terms Patanjali uses. He is hinting that this is no ordinary text but rather an authoritative treatise on the knowledge and practice of yoga.

In the *Sutras*, Patanjali draws from thousands of years of yoga knowledge and practice. He was certainly familiar with the *Bhagavad-gita*, the most important and famous text on yoga, spoken by Krishna, and also with the spiritual philosophy of the *Upanishads*. And he was schooled in Sankhya, another classical Indic school of knowledge of reality and consciousness.

Patanjali wrote the *Sutras* at a time when Buddhism was prevalent in India, and he is also indirectly refuting some of their claims.

In short, this is a serious textbook on the philosophy and practice of yoga by a learned and experienced master.

2. Yoga means controlling the fluctuations of the mind.

If the whole idea of writing a sutra treatise is to be concise, why not summarize the whole book in a few words? That's what Patanjali does here by defining yoga in three words—*mind*, *turnings*, and *control*—making this the most important sutra in the book.

Yoga is all about the mind. Our whole life experience is dependent on our mind, not on external reality. Neurologists will confirm this fact, though they reject the word *mind* and speak of the brain instead. It is this mind/brain that creates an interpretation of physical reality. Even basic things like colors, smells, and sounds are but creations of our brains and, further, at any given moment we are interpreting only a small slice of our surrounding reality. It can all get weird and somewhat disturbing, like some sci-fi horror movie in which you discover that you're living in a pod connected to a computer. But the indisputable fact is that the state of our mind is the determining factor of the quality and outcome of our life.

This is the great gift of yoga: to teach us that we can control our mind and that in so doing we can achieve states of increasing bliss and peace, regardless of external reality.

In *The 3T Path*, I laid out how this can be achieved in an easy, systematic way:

Yoga is a holistic path of self-improvement and self-realization with five major avenues of perfection, plus lifestyle suggestions to guarantee progress.

It all starts with *jnana*, knowledge or wisdom. An encounter with a spiritual master and the study of yoga books such as the *Yoga Sutras*, the *Bhagavad-gita*, the *Upanishads*, and *Srimad-Bhagavatam* provide the basis for advancement. Yoga is firmly grounded in knowledge of the world around us, metaphysical reality, consciousness, and the nature of God. This is presented as a spiritual science in the form of practices and techniques that deliver specific results and in an internally consistent body of philosophy. In short, yoga is a path of self-improvement and self-realization that makes sense and works.

With this *jnana*, the yogi is guided to the highest aspect of yoga, *bhakti*. *Bhakti* is a special Sanskrit word for devotion. It is identified in the *Yoga Sutras* as the perfection of *samadhi* (Sutra 2.45), the highest aspect of yogic perfection. Similarly, in the *Bhagavad-gita* Krishna says that *bhakti* is the highest form of yoga and the key ingredient to spiritual perfection. *Srimad-Bhagavatam* is almost entirely dedicated to explaining the different forms of devotion and the different forms of God, to emphasize that *bhakti* is the highest expression of spiritual existence, with Krishna as its topmost object. Because *bhakti* is the highest aspect of yoga, it can also be the most difficult to experience and even understand. This is why many, even among the yoga community, are uninterested or put off by deep *Krishna-bhakti*, for it requires serious study (*jnana*), specialized daily meditational practices, and profound changes in one's worldview.

Jnana and *bhakti* constitute the spiritual component of yoga. There are three other components, or avenues of perfection, that assist the yogi to achieve self-improvement, bringing immediate results in well-being – mindfulness, *dharma*, and inner peace.

Mindfulness is a modern term for a key aspect of this ancient yoga practice. In short, it means to be aware, to be conscious of your consciousness, and to be able to experience a thought, sensation, or external action with your full attention. More importantly, it means to be in the here and now, resisting one's mind's urge to drift into the past in lamentation or skip to the future, fantasizing about what it would take to finally be happy. The real key to happiness, it turns out, is to just live life, right now. The trick is to train your brain to focus on what you're doing at any given moment, to focus as much as possible on your actions and not the result of your actions.

This brings us to the next key avenue of perfection: *dharma*. The obvious question that arises in regard to focus is, "What action should we focus our mind *on?*" *Dharma* is a rich concept, and the word has many meanings, but the main focus is on *dharma* as that which needs to be done – essence and duty. Duty can be imposed; essence cannot. *Dharma* is thus that duty born of who you truly are, of your nature. It's not an external or social imposition; it's what you need to do at any given moment to be the best person you can be. It's doing the right thing at the right time. Being *dharmic* is more than just doing good or avoiding hurtful or violent behavior, though that is certainly included in the concept. And it can't be boiled down to a list of do's and don'ts or things to be avoided. *Dharma* is fluid and alive and sensitive to different aspects of your life. Major changes to your *dharma* can occur from one moment to the next.

One way to understand *dharma* is to rephrase the classic line "Don't ask what your country can do for you; ask what you can do for your country." Dharma is that action which is required of you, from one moment to the next, to best fulfill who you truly are.

The final avenue of perfection is finding inner peace: creating internal harmony and balance through awareness and control of one's emotions, motivations, and desires. This involves putting into practice techniques confirmed by psychology and neuroscience to increase positivity and decrease negative emotions. Of the many positive emotions, gratitude takes primacy. Its positive effects on well-being have been richly documented by science. Of the negative emotions to be curtailed, anger is the most destructive. We have the power to actively cultivate our internal state of mind, to guarantee greater clarity and joy.

These five avenues of perfection—mindfulness, *dharma*, inner peace, *jnana*, and *bhakti*—require conscious, daily, and active effort, but they will richly reward those who invest in them. And they are mutually supportive—advancement in one helps advancement in the others. The transformational power of applying yourself to these five avenues of perfection in nothing short of miraculous.

All five of these avenues of perfection are about the mind—your focus, your effort to remain true to yourself, your mental map or worldview. But yogis were aware of the mind-body loop. What your mind does affects your body, and what happens to your body affects your mind. So, along with information about the mind and techniques to enhance our mental state, which fall in these five avenues of perfection of the 3T Path, there are important lifestyle suggestions.

Patanjali will mention (among others) cleanliness, non-violence, sexual restraint, and simplicity as necessary and core aspects of yoga practice. This implies that a serious yogi should adopt such crucial lifestyle choices as having a plant-based diet, sobriety, chastity, cleanliness, and a life free of consumerism and clutter. These and other lifestyle suggestions enhance mental peace and clarity and maximize our potential to advance in the five avenues.

3. Then the seer becomes absorbed in his or her true nature.

What happens when the mind is fully controlled in yoga?

Is the final goal of yoga to simply cease to exist? Is it to stop thinking and become devoid of consciousness, like a rock or log? No, Patanjali explains; what happens is that you finally get to be yourself—your eternal true self.

Patanjali chose the term *seer* to identify the self, to emphasize the continuance of cognition, to make it clear that the goal in yoga is to purify and to optimize our state of conscious existence, not to destroy it or reduce it to nil.

In the *Bhagavad-gita* Krishna makes this even clearer, explaining the eternal nature of the soul and emphasizing that the perfection of yoga is to go to Him, to exist eternally in pure consciousness in another realm, beyond matter—His abode.

Yoga embraces life, consciousness, and love. The goal of yoga is to remove the obstacles to attaining perfection in these, in order to live beautifully. The problem is not with life, not with having consciousness,  but with those things that take us away from experiencing our true nature. Yoga can clear away mental processes and habits that cover our consciousness and our true eternal, non-material, nature.

4. Otherwise, the seer will identify with the fluctuations of the mind.

It's all too easy to identify with the meaning of this sutra. When we're not in yoga, we identify with whatever our mind is throwing at us. We live the life it cooks up, influenced by our past experiences, peer pressure, advertising, and endless desires to satisfy our material senses and, most importantly, wrongfully identifying ourselves with our bodies, unaware of our true eternal nature, the existence and nature of God, and the existence of a transcendental realm beyond matter.

As a result, we limit ourselves. We ignore our ability to shape our life experience beyond what we are given by external circumstances. Or worse, we ignore our full potential to go beyond this life and the experiences available on the mundane platform.

5. There are five categories of mental fluctuations, and they are either troublesome or not.

This sutra marks the beginning of a section on mental fluctuations. Consider this section an analytical description of our minds. A lot of the *Yoga Sutras* reads as a treatise on psychology.

The section begins by stating that the functions, or fluctuations, of the mind will be presented in five basic categories. More importantly, all five of them are double-edged swords. In other words, any of your mental states can be adjusted and will be either useful or detrimental to your enlightenment, your progress in yoga.

So, the good news is that you already have everything you need to progress in yoga. The bad news is that you have to be constantly vigilant. As Patanjali states later, at every moment you are either advancing or retreating in your path to blissful enlightenment—there is no middle ground and no timeout.

6. The five categories are 1) perceiving things correctly, 2) perceiving things incorrectly, 3) imagining, 4) sleeping, and 5) remembering.

Patanjali separates our mental states into five simple categories. Any other mental function would be included in one of these.

7. Things can be correctly perceived by direct sense perception, logic, and/or a trustworthy source.

How can you judge the veracity of what you know? This list of three valid means of attaining correct information is universally accepted in Indic philosophy, not just by the yoga tradition, much less Patanjali.

The list is ordered from worst to best. Direct sense perception is the most fallible way of perceiving what something is, logic gives better results, and information from an expert, authority, or perfectly reliable witness is best.

Direct sense perception is subject to error. How big is the sun? You look up, and it doesn't look so big. In an eclipse, we perceive the moon being as big as the sun. The classic case of a mirage, when heat distorts the air and makes it look like water from a distance, is another example. Magic shows are based on our failure to perceive things directly. Movies and photoshopped pictures use other ways to fool our senses.

Logic is more reliable. Every day, the sun rises in the east and sets in the west, so one can conclude that it will continue to repeat the pattern. Mountains are solid and unmoving, and birds fly. So, we know that a bird will move about but mountains and hills will not. Everybody dies, so I know that I'll die too.

An expert or authoritative source is the most reliable. We naturally trust the word of doctors and scientists, as well as the testimony of our close family members and friends. Someone experienced and trustworthy can give us solid information we cannot otherwise attain.

This type of evidence is extended to, and especially meant for, the sacred literature in the yoga tradition. Texts such as the *Upanishads*, the *Bhagavad-gita*, and the *Yoga Sutras* are authoritative sources of the highest order. Their content is accepted by teachers in the yoga tradition to be reliable and correct. Millions of practitioners over thousands of years—including myself—have experienced the trustworthiness of these texts.

8. Things are perceived incorrectly by false knowledge.

Our perception of reality is filtered, colored, and distorted by both our past experiences and current focus. Research has shown that we experience a highly selective view of reality. The first step in dealing with this is to become aware of it.

In psychology, the term used to describe this is "inattentional blindness." The most famous experiment, which became a big YouTube hit, showed how people would fail to spot a person dressed in a gorilla costume passing right in front of the camera, because they were focused on counting the number of times people were passing a basketball to each other.

If we can't see a person dressed as a gorilla right in front of us, imagine how much more is going unperceived around us.

This happens because our brain has energy-saving mechanisms. Processing information is hard work, so our brain pre-selects what it will process, significantly reducing the amount of data it must process. Think of it as a spam filter. Just as your email program automatically separates emails it thinks you don't want to see, making it easier for you to deal with your inbox, so too your brain shows you only the part of reality you need to be aware of. And just as you're not aware of what your spam filter is doing and what rules are in play, so too you are not aware of the exact filters in operation and what information is being hidden from you by your brain.

You can, however, change this. You can learn how rules are created by your unconscious filters. Your filters are determined by your conscious objectives and current worldview, or, to use another important psychological term, your mental map.

The participants in the gorilla experiment had the conscious objective of counting the number of times a ball was passed. This focus created a filter. The instruction, if verbalized, would sound something like, "Dear brain, all I want to know is how many times the ball is passed from one team member to another. Don't tell me anything else." The brain then dutifully performs the task. As a result, most participants never "saw" the gorilla, even though it was right in front of them.

When we're in a bad mood, we create a filter of negativity. We tell our brain, "Dear brain, I'm in a foul mood. The world is conspiring against me. Please show me how I'm right about this. Help me prove to myself and the world how life is miserable, by pointing out to me everything that is wrong." The brain then carefully helps us see problems and hopelessness everywhere, making us even more miserable, more entrenched in that worldview, which then further strengthens our negativity filter.

But we can hack the system. It's as if we can click on our "configurations" and take manual override of the filters. One documented example of this is the use of gratitude journals. A gratitude journal is the simple exercise of every day writing down three to five things for which we are grateful. This may sound insignificant, but studies show it has a remarkable effect on uplifting people's well-being. Why? Because a new filter is put into action: "Dear brain, I have to write down things I'm grateful for. So I'm looking for good things in my life for which I can give thanks. Please record positive moments in my day so I have something to write in my gratitude journal." Now, as you go about life, you start to notice the good things. This makes you more positive. As you become more positive, you see more good things and interpret more of them as being positive, and so on.

On a larger scale, we have to bring to our conscious attention important considerations on life: Who am I? Where am I? What is the goal of my life? Is there more to reality than meets the eye? Does God exist?

These existential questions aren't mere curiosities. They are not just nice quandaries to mull over in a philosophy class or over a campfire with friends. They are pillars of how we perceive reality and, as such, define our filters, which in turn define our life experience and well-being. Whether or not you are aware of it, you have an ongoing answer to these questions and they are shaping your life, your choices, and your mental map.

When these pillars of our identity and worldview are wrong, we perceive reality wrongly, and consequently we suffer.

9. Imagination is the result of using words without a real object.

We can distinguish two categories in this third function of the mind: 1) metaphors and 2) creative use of our experiences.

Metaphors are figures of speech that help us understand life. One classic example is Shakespeare's line "All the world's a stage, and all the men and women merely players." The world isn't actually a stage and we are not really all actors, but Shakespeare is making a comparison that is both intelligible and useful.

The second use of this mental function is one we often engage in all too often: creating alternative realities in our mind, based on our experiences. We have seen mountains and we have seen gold, and so we can imagine mountains of gold.

Consciously or unconsciously, we imagine our future with every choice we make. When you decide whether to paint your room yellow or green, you are picturing what each would look like, and based on your vision, you are thus able to experience what each would feel like.

Research shows that our bodies react on many levels to choices. You salivate upon being given the choice to eat something delicious. You feel your stomach tighten when you think of something nauseating. Our choices aren't based on cold calculations, though they may seem so to us. Our processes for making choices are visceral and reflect physiological reactions, sometimes unperceivable to our awareness but nonetheless registered by our unconscious, thus swaying the outcome.

In *The 3T Path*, I point out that the root of all our suffering is based on the unrestricted use of this ability. We become lost in a fantasy paradigm, constantly reassessing how our future should be to the extent that we miss out on the present, on life happening right now. This focus on how life should be instead on how it *is* generates unlimited desires, resulting in endless anxiety, frustration, and despondency.

10. Sleep is experience of non-real things.

In sleep, we experience all kinds of situations, but there is no question of discussing whether they are correctly or incorrectly perceived; the experience itself is the only real thing. Even deep, dreamless sleep is itself an experience, since you wake up and feel refreshed and renewed from it.

Dreams are an opportunity to look into your unconscious. Self-observation is an integral part of the path of yoga. The better you know yourself, the more you can fine-tune your mental functions to maximize your potential and avoid pitfalls. As soon as you wake up, try to hold onto your dream experience for a minute or two—see what you can get from it and what you can learn about yourself.

In *Srimad-Bhagavatam* the great cosmic sage Narada Muni describes a special type of dream yogis have in which they burn up karma by quickly absorbing the lessons of what in their waking states would have been experiences lasting many years. A yogi might experience an entire marriage in one night's sleep and take in the deep realizations that would come from that. Or one might experience living in great luxury and awaken with the deep realization that such superficial pleasures mean nothing to the soul. These are real experiences the person had coming to him or her in the form of "seed-karma" to be lived in this or another life, but they fructify and are experienced in the subtle realm of sleep, sparing the yogi from having to prolong his or her incarnate existence.

In an even more esoteric text, the *Caitanya-caritamrta*, we find an even rarer type of dream, in which God Himself appears to a great soul to give him direct instruction, usually in the form of a specific mission to be accomplished.

Many spiritual practitioners have experienced visions of God and guru in their dreams, though, based on my own experience, in almost every case these are most likely just the dreamer's unconscious self using that image figuratively.

Dreams are often mentioned in sacred literature for another purpose: to point out how easily we fully accept illusion as reality. Every night, we live out dreams rich in all kinds of experiences, from love to terror, with animals, people, things, and places. And in our sleep, we accept that experience as reality. It's only when we wake up that we realize that our dreams were not real, that our awakened state is clearer and brighter and that it makes more sense.

Well, just as we wake up every day from a dream reality to our regular mundane awakened state, so too when we practice yoga we are able to awaken again to the ultimate state of existence: transcendental reality. Just as, upon waking, you realize how illusory your dream was, so too, upon becoming spiritually awakened, you will realize the illusory nature of mundane life and that there is another level of reality, the transcendental realm, known in the West as "the Kingdom of God." It is the ultimate level of reality beyond the dream-like mundane existence we experience in our material bodies. If this is hard to accept, you need look no further than last night's dream to remind yourself how easily you accept illusion as reality, over and over again.

Another important realization to be taken from dreams is that of our ultimate existence beyond matter, be it in dream, deep sleep, or our mundane awakened state. According to *Srimad-Bhagavatam*, "By remembering and contemplating the succession of wakefulness, dreaming and deep sleep, the living entity can understand that he is one throughout the three stages of consciousness and is transcendental" (11.13.32). You'll find that transcendental consciousness is referred to "the fourth state," the fourth and final stage of consciousness.

Some traditional commentaries on the *Yoga Sutras* consider that this fourth mental fluctuation refers exclusively to deep dreamless sleep, the mental experience of not having any experience. They suggest that dreams are a sub-category of the next and final mental function: memory. But dreams are unlike the correct or incorrect perception of reality, and they differ from imagination. They offer us a different experience of an alternative reality. This, in turn, provides us with valid realizations and useful knowledge, which then become a part of who we are and help shape how we view and interpret life. They are not akin to merely remembering past events in our life.

11. Memory is the retention of the experiences of previously perceived objects.

Your mind is constantly changing. Every event, every experience, and every thought changes who you are. Whether you retain a vivid memory of an experience or not, your mind is changed by every moment of existence and every input, sometimes dramatically, most times imperceptibly. This is supported not only by the yoga tradition, but also by neuroscience.

The greatest danger memory can offer us is in the form of lamentation. All too often, we become victims of our past traumas, unable to process them positively for our growth. Emotions become buried, which can lead to physical and mental ailments.

Our mental map can become distorted by trauma. We hold on to a traumatic experience and redefine our self-image and worldview, tinging reality negatively because of our experience. This impacts our well-being, strengthening negative emotions such as depression, hopelessness, and anger. We salt the earth of our garden of inner peace, preventing positive emotions from taking root.

We have the ability to not only overcome trauma, but to grow from it. The term for this is "post-traumatic growth." Those who grow from a trauma can find opportunities. They think in a forward manner and don't get stuck in lamenting what has occurred. It's not a question of ignoring the pain or denying the event; it's about accepting what has happened and using the power of the experience to reach new heights and discover untapped resources in ourselves.

Memory should make us wise. We can learn from our mistakes, and, let's face it, we make mistakes every day. But to learn from them, we have to stop and reflect. We have to insert time into our daily schedule to contemplate our actions, emotions, and motivations, as well as how they affect our well-being. This will not only help you know yourself better; it will help you make the most of what you've lived so far.

Memory has the power to reinforce a specific experience or mindset. When you consciously remember what your values are, you reinforce your dedication to remain true to them. When you remember the importance of your meaningful relationships, you find the determination to give them the energy they deserve. And when you remember your spiritual goals and identity—and God—you strengthen your resolve to stick to the path of yoga and invest in your higher self.

12. You can pacify the fluctuations of the mind by practice and detachment.

This *sutra* is Patanjali's first suggestion of how to practice yoga. He lays out two foundational concepts: practice and detachment, both of which are mentioned by Krishna in the *Bhagavad-gita* (6.35).

Practice in yoga is called *sadhana*. The details of which will be presented in the second chapter. In *The 3T Path* I lay out a comprehensive guide to this practice, with a further, more specific, daily spiritual practice. Without daily practice, without *sadhana*, there is no question of advancing in yoga.

Detachment is a crucial quality on the yoga path. That might sound cold, like we just don't care. But detachment is the ability to accept reality as it is and focus on your actions, not the reactions you experience. Detachment means you're focused on the internal, not the external, on your own state of mind, your goals, your motivations, and your deeds. Detachment arises from the realization that you can control only yourself, your thoughts, and your actions, not the rest of the world and certainly not others or how they act. We should focus on what we can control. Our happiness is determined by us, by how well we're acting, not by those things beyond our control.

Detachment doesn't mean you don't care or, worse, that you cannot love. On the contrary, you cannot love if you're not detached. Detachment gives you the freedom to love purely, solely interested in what's best for the one you love. To whatever degree you're not detached, to that degree you cannot love purely. Your expectations of a return for your love and service tarnish the relationship.

Lastly, detachment gives you freedom to transform, to live the new and brighter version of yourself being chiseled out by your *sadhana*. If you want to grow and expand your consciousness, be prepared to change. A lot will change! Your habits, including your diet, sobriety, and views on sex, will change, and, with that, you'll find yourself gravitating to new social scenes, new goals in life, maybe a new career. But for all that to happen, you have to be detached from what's going on in your life now.

13. Practice means putting in effort to steady the mind.

Yoga requires practice, and practice means putting effort toward the goal of controlling the fluctuations of the mind. Research shows that we have over seventy thousand thoughts a day. Anyone who has sat down to meditate knows just how hard it is to pacify the mind. Even Arjuna, who hears the *Bhagavad-gita* from Krishna, remarks that he thinks controlling the mind is more difficult than controlling the wind. Is there an easy fix? Sadly, no. Effort is required. The good news is that we can experience the benefits at every step. And even a slightly more pacified mind is better than one in turmoil.

To make the mind steadfast and peaceful, we need to put to use all the tools we can get our hands on. We have to work from different angles, as I recommend in *The 3T Path*. From diet to meditation, from work to leisure, from mindfulness to *bhakti*, at every moment you can apply a different combination of techniques to advance in yoga.

14. This practice is well established when it's performed very well, uninterruptedly, and for a very long time.

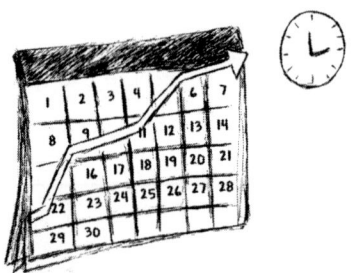

I've long been attracted by the practicality of yoga. The simple message is that you get what you deserve. You want to advance? Work on it! Here are the specifics:

First, it has to be done right. Take the time to learn what's required of you and then practice with love and with attention to detail. Embrace your practice with determination. Apply the Kaizen principle: try every day to do it just a little bit better. Every time you meditate, try to meditate with just a little more focus. Every day, try to be a little more attuned to your dharma, a little more in the here and now. Try to experience more *bhakti* and make God just a little more present in your life. Constantly seeking to do it just a little bit better gives joy to your life, and over time, one can make remarkable progress.

Second, you can't stop. Life is your field of yoga practice. You live in yoga. This is not a religion for you to remember on Sundays or in rites of passage. This is not an exercise for Tuesdays and Thursdays in the evening. Yoga is fine-tuning your brain to live better at every moment. Everything that comes your way, everything you're doing, is there for you to practice and advance in yoga.

Lastly, be patient. It's going to take time. In the *Bhagavad-gita*, Krishna talks about it taking lifetimes! But before you become discouraged, remember that Krishna also says that it's joyfully practiced. Every moment you're at your best, whatever that best may be for now, is a good moment. You'll feel the joy, the reward, of achieving your top potential. And then it keeps getting better. As you progress, no matter how slowly, you achieve higher and higher levels of well-being, strength, focus, and joy.

But take heed—if you stop your practice, you will not coast along; you'll slide down. Our painful past habits, vices, egoism, and attachments will rise again. Until you find yourself truly liberated and no longer inhabiting a material body in this universe, you're not out of the woods. Both sacred literature and the story of famous gurus in the last fifty years show this to be the case. No matter how advanced he or she is, how much charisma he or she has, or how much power he or she has gained over lifetimes of practice, if a yogi drops his or her guard, the old weeds of ignorance grow back.

15. Detachment is the mental power to resist hankering after sense objects, perceived or described.

I'll never forget a conversation I had with a great *bhakti*-yogi Sridhar Maharaja, disciple of the legendary master Swami Prabhupada. He was a renunciate and had just come from Rio de Janeiro, famous for its beaches full of beautiful women wearing tiny bikinis, and I was fortunate enough to be hosting him in my house in Brasília, Brazil. I was just starting my spiritual life, and along with my curiosity, I was quite clueless and lacked good etiquette. So, I asked him how he felt seeing all those women and if that didn't disturb him. He laughed and answered, "I have red blood in my veins." He went on to explain that though their beauty and attraction registered in his mind, there was no hankering for sex. The sense object was registered, but no desire for action ensued. You don't become blind, I now understand; you just become wiser. You know better.

Real detachment comes not from isolating yourself from sense objects, by locking yourself away in an ashram or cave. It comes not from hating sense objects, as you can see in immature male renunciates who despise women. Real detachment comes from understanding the pros and cons of any sensory experience, and understanding that the cons always outweigh the pros. It's not artificial repression; it's a calm realization of things to come and of the true cost of going out of your *dharma* in the name of sensory pleasure. Supporting this mentality is the constantly experienced and real pleasure of satisfying your true nature.

I've learned that there are basically two things that really satisfy the true you: service and connection.

I often remind myself of Saint Mother Teresa's saying: "The fruit of prayer is love, and the fruit of love is service." Service is love in action. Love has no meaning if it's not conducive to doing something for the loved one.

Everything you do can be done in the spirit of love. Every action can be an expression of your desire to serve someone else and serve yourself in the sense of preserving your physical and mental well-being. The details of what this service implies is revealed by your *dharma*.

When you treat people as people, not objects or machines to satisfy your needs, you experience the feeling of connection. Even the smallest exchanges, like saying good morning to someone in an elevator, are opportunities to connect and experience that soul-to-soul link—deeper and more meaningful relationships even more so.

Swami Prabhupada summed it up nicely when he said that people want someone to love and something to do.

As you learn to live life experiencing the deep pleasure and satisfaction of serving and connecting, the attraction to get pleasure from the outside, through sensory enjoyment, diminishes proportionally. You soon come to the point of being satisfied with the pleasure that comes naturally in the execution of your *dharma*. You become fulfilled with the simple yet profound act of living truly. This is detachment.

16. Beyond detachment comes complete indifference to material life. This is born through direct perception of the personal soul.

This sutra describes spiritual perfection. As we progress in yoga, we come to experience our true spiritual nature. We live and feel as souls and not as material bodies. Advancement brings the realization that our personal nature—our values, goals, and ability to love, think, and choose—does not stem from our bodies, nor from our brains, but from our eternal non-material selves. This is the direct perception of the personal soul.

Once you understand and experience your true spiritual nature, you no longer require material existence. You naturally outgrow the need for a material body and have long since stopped yearning for mundane situations or pleasures. You no longer need the artificial, illusory, experience of life in the universe, because you're already experiencing your true life beyond it.

This sutra is stating that control of the mind, the practice of yoga, is surpassed when you are no longer involved with material life. At this stage, you no longer see yourself as your body or think that life requires matter, having understood and experienced that life exists on another level: pure transcendence. The yogi awakens to a life of pure loving dealings with other pure souls and the Supreme Soul, God, in a realm beyond this universe. Just as your dream is broken when you wake up and remember your identity, so too the dream/nightmare of mundane life is broken when we remember fully our true personal spiritual existence.

17. The four stages of achieving perfect focus (*samadhi*) are: 1) focus on matter, 2) focus on the subtle aspect of matter,

3) focus on the ability to perceive reality and 4) focus on existence, in the experience of "I am."

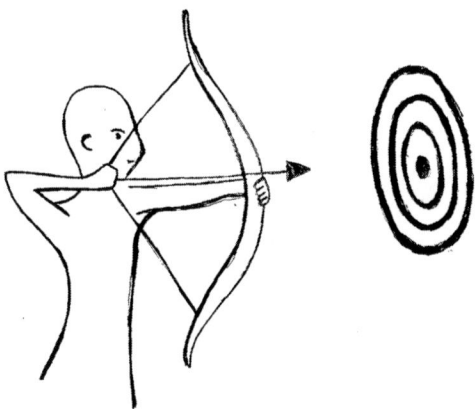

What you focus on determines the quality of your life. Here's a brief description of the different levels of focus you can achieve:

No focus is to be "in your head" in the sense of that tiresome rumination of past events, future concerns, petty issues, and the actions of others. A 2010 Harvard study showed that a distracted mind is an unhappy mind. Without focus, the mind is lost in time and space, jumping from one thing to another by association, without any discernible benefit.

The first level of focus is on your job at hand. Focus on physical reality right in front of you. This is the big step, and it's one of the key concepts in the 3T Path. Bring your attention to the best you can do right now. If it's riding a bike, ride the bike mindfully. Experience it completely. If it's writing a business proposal, do that. Whatever you're doing, bring your mind with you. All of it. This brings an immediate sense of well-being. Tens of thousands of studies confirm the positive impact and effectiveness of mindfulness. Even the first few minutes of practice gives you direct perception of its usefulness.

The second level is to be able to focus on the experience, on the metaphysical reality of what is happening in your life. It's about adding a new layer of focus. Let's take the example of walking. Zero focus means walking without paying attention to the act of walking. You're "spacing out"; thoughts flying every which way. You'll be lucky if you don't trip and fall, get run over, or walk into a lamp post. The first level of focus is to walk mindfully. You bring your attention to the act of walking, to the here and now. You're attentively placing one foot at a time forward and being conscious of your body and your settings. This second level is to focus, additionally, on the *experience* of mindful walking. How does it feel? Explore that sensation, that state of mind.

Explore your ability to invoke feelings and emotions at will, without them being triggered by real or imagined events. Use your focusing ability, your mindfulness training, to examine your state of mind, to be constantly aware of the inner garden of your emotions and motivations. In *The 3T Path*, I call this avenue of perfection "inner peace" – the ability to monitor, perceive, and shape the subtle reality of our psychology.

The third level is to become aware of your ability to realize levels one and two. In other words, to be able to focus on your perception of reality, both internal and external. Be mindful that you are observing, seeing. With this realization, you can understand that you are not your thoughts or emotions. You need not identify with any thought or emotion going through your head. It's not you. Be aware of your thoughts and emotions, but let them go. Give yourself planned sessions of psychological exploration, to examine and identify trapped emotions from the past, from when you were mistakenly identifying with your emotions. Go over major events and relationships in your life, and examine the feelings they invoke to make sure you can let them go now. Get rid of that useless and painful baggage.

Lastly, become aware of that you exist purely. *Cogito ergo sum*, the philosopher Descartes famously concluded. "I think therefore I am." Beyond all matter, beyond even the ability to perceive matter, you can experience your eternal existence. You are consciousness. With the power of consciousness, you become conscious of anything on which you can focus, but more importantly, be aware, simply, that you *are*. Patanjali uses the term "I am-ness": the state of being aware of existing.

18. Another way is to practice terminating all fluctuations of the mind, at which time only subliminal impressions remain.

There are two paths in yoga: that of the enlightened life and that of pure meditation.

The path of enlightened life consists living a "normal" life of work, home, family, friends, and community, but in the practice of controlling and directing the mind, in yoga. This means having a *dharmic* life in divine connection in the here and now. Or, to use Krishna's words in the *Bhagavad-gita*, a life "as an offering unto Me." The path of enlightened life is clearly the main recommendation in the *Bhagavad-gita* and *Srimad-Bhagavatam*. In *The 3T Path*, I detail this process in its many facets.

The other path is that of pure meditation. In the *Bhagavad-gita* it is called *dhyana-yoga*. Here in the *Yoga Sutras*, it's described as *astanga-yoga*, the eight-limbed path of yoga. A good portion of the *Yoga Sutras* is devoted to this practice. For it, the yogi has to forego "normal" life. Even to this day, you'll find yogis living in caves or in the wilderness, close to a sacred river, away from civilization. In this path, the yogi must spend all day, for the rest of his or her life, in meditation, interrupting it only to eat meager raw wild foods and to get some sleep. Due to the arduous nature of this practice, almost no one takes to it. These days, the practice is practically extinct. In ancient times, yogis would meditate for so long and so intensely that they would achieve the power to manipulate matter with their minds. These superpowers will be described in the third chapter.

I mention this here because one interpretation of these two *sutras*, 1.17 and 1.18, is that one refers to the path of exclusive meditation and the other to the constant practice of living an enlightened life. In one, *samadhi* is achieved by the ever finer focus of the mind; in the other, it is achieved by the constant practice of trying to live more and more in yoga at every moment.

19. Some attain full focus on the subtle aspects of material reality and live a disembodied existence.

Some background about the soul and of material nature is necessary to better understand this *sutra*.

In the Vedic viewpoint, life is the symptom of the soul and has nothing to do with matter. Souls assume bodies due to their fluctuations, but at no point is the existence of the soul dependent on the body. It's the other way around. The body needs the presence of the soul to exist. Without the soul, the body starts to decompose and merge back with nature. Before attaining spiritual perfection, the soul can experience life only in one body or another. When the term of one body is finished, the soul must carry on in another body.

Bodies are made of material energy, but material energy is not so simple. As modern scientists have found, material nature can exist in subtle forms, which are far removed from the "solid" manifestations of reality such as stones and logs, earth, wind, and fire. Krishna explains in the *Bhagavad-gita* that super-subtle elements of reality exist in the form of what we translate as mind, intelligence, and false ego. These are not just concepts; they are real elements of physical reality, just like water. Of course, this is all very hard to conceptualize, because it goes way beyond our direct sensory experience. You can't smell, see, hear, or touch mind, intelligence, or false ego. The best you can hope for is to perceive the existence of these subtle elements, because you do have mind, intelligence, and false ego right now.

Ether is the finest aspect of nature still perceived by our regular senses. It can be translated as "vacuum," and you can perceive it by the space it takes up. If there is a perfect vacuum inside a bottle, you can measure the space the vacuum takes up. Mind is finer and cannot be measured in any way. Intelligence is finer than the mind, and false ego is the subtlest aspect of reality. False ego is the soul's identification with matter. Intelligence is how to explore and interpret the world in that identification. For that, it requires a mind to coordinate the senses and thoughts, which then requires a physical body to interact with denser material reality: solids, liquids, radiant energy, gases, and vacuum.

Bodies are thus composed of all of the elements of material nature, from false ego to solids. But not all bodies are like this.

Ghosts, for example, have bodies made of only the subtle elements of mind, intelligence, and false ego. That's why you normally can't see them and they can't touch anything but can go through walls, float around, etc.

Other cosmic creatures exist in similar subtle, or disembodied, forms—even bodies made exclusively of intelligence and false ego.

What this sutra is stating is that a yogi might inadvertently become stuck in such a body if, when following the meditation-only path of yoga, he or she focuses his or her mind entirely on such a subtle aspect of material energy, instead of on its true spiritual form. The yoga tradition goes as far as to state how long such a state would last, according to the subtle element of matter on which the soul fixes its consciousness. Those who fix their minds on intelligence for example, merging into it, would remain in such a state for 100 thousand Manu periods. A Manu period is 310 million Earth years, so such a yogi would remain in such a state for 31 trillion years—a very peaceful 31 trillion years, to be sure, but not the final goal of yoga. Such a yogi would eventually have to return to a gross physical body and try again.

20. Perfection is attained by faith, vigorous endeavor, memory, trance, and discernment.

Whether the yogi is following the path of an enlightened life or of pure meditation, Patanjali suggests that there are five elements, or steps, in doing so.

First comes faith. Anything we do requires faith. We can't get out of bed if we do not have faith that doing so will be better than staying in bed. Faith here is used in the sense of choosing our course of action in the belief it will give us the intended results. This faith gives us the clarity of mind to know what we want and what our strategy will be.

Once a life path has been chosen, we need to apply ourselves to it with vigor and prowess. The greater the goal, the greater the need for grit. Half-measures won't cut it. And the goal of yoga is the greatest of all—ultimate bliss and eternal freedom from all suffering! It's pretty lofty stuff, and it won't come cheap. But it will come if we apply ourselves to it with determination and strength.

Memory here means keeping the goal in mind. In yoga, the biggest challenge is to keep trying, moment by moment. Our tendency is to fall asleep at the wheel and drift along life in forgetfulness of our ultimate spiritual nature and objectives. In the language of the 3T Path, we easily slip back into the Fantasy Paradigm, losing out on reality. Our minds are conditioned to live in lamentation or anxiety, and it takes a lot of effort to keep bringing the mind back to the here and now, to your dharma, to your spiritual identity and God. In the Bible, we find the recommendation to "watch and pray." If you're alert, "watching," remembering your yogic goal, you can advance.

With the three previous elements in play, you can then experience *samadhi*, trance, or full absorption in your divine nature.

Finally, as you accumulate moments of *samadhi*, you'll one day reach the finish line: *viveka*—discernment—which here means the ultimate ability to differentiate your true spiritual nature from matter, or, to use the Sanskrit terms, distinguish *purusa* from *prakrti*. At this point, you no longer need to be in a material body of any kind and thus need not live in the material world ever again. You're ready to resume life in God's abode of pure transcendental reality.

21. For those who practice with intensity, the goal is near.

22. How near it is depends on the level of practice, be it mild, moderate, or extreme.

One of the beautiful aspects of yoga spirituality is just how practical and down-to-earth it is. It's not a question of beliefs and hopes alone. Your advancement is measured by the degree to which you are keeping your mind under control and living out your true nature, moment by moment. The result is clearly experienced. You live out your yoga practice. How much time did you spend in the here and now? To how much hankering and lamenting are you falling prey? How conscious were you throughout the day of your nature as a non-material eternal entity? How much equanimity are you experiencing? Are you seeing all living beings as equal to you? How connected were you to God throughout the day? These are practical pointers of your advancement, which you can evaluate and on which you can work harder to advance further.

23. Perfection is achieved by devotion to the Lord.

Though Patanjali did not set out to give elaborate theology in his *Yoga Sutras*, leaving that for texts such as the *Bhagavad-gita* and *Srimad-Bhagavatam*, he nonetheless emphasized the final goal of yoga and the most powerful yoga technique: *bhakti*, devotion to the Lord. Perfection in yoga is achieved by a combination of one's own endeavors and the grace of God. If you do nothing, you'll achieve no spiritual progress. But it's contradictory to speak of seeking spiritual perfection without God, as spiritual perfection means to attain the state of connection (yoga) with God.

Here are some other reasons why *bhakti* is so important:

1. As Krishna explains in the *Bhagavad-gita*, we are all parts of Him. To understand our true ultimate nature, we must understand God.
2. God, by definition, controls everything. If we want to overcome the influence of illusion and control our mind, it behooves us to ask for help of He who has full control over these.
3. All knowledge and ability come from God. If we want the ability and knowledge to advance in yoga, these will necessarily come from God anyway, so it's more loving and effective if we ask for them personally.
4. *Bhakti* is the only aspect of yoga practice that we will continue to experience beyond our material body and physical existence in the universe.
5. We saw in Sutra 1.19 the danger of missing the mark and meditating on something other than pure spirit. When we meditate on God – His holy name, instructions, actions, and form – there is no such danger, as these are, by definition, purely spiritual. *Bhakti* thus grants immediate and high-level yoga practice, regardless of previous advancement.

All other practices, including lifestyle choices in and around yoga, exist to support and advance *bhakti*. And *bhakti* helps all other practices.

24. The Lord is unique—untouched by trouble, karma, the results of karma, and unconscious behavioral influences.

There are two major mistaken conclusions we may reach about God: 1) God does not exist, and 2) we are God because God is just energy (*brahman*, source energy, divine light, etc.), just as we are.

That God exists is taken for granted in the yoga tradition. Yoga exists as a means of understanding and reaching God. The need for God is explained rationally. The nature, attributes, and special position of God are also fully explained.

The second mistake, of confusing the soul to be God, is here addressed. Any yogi can understand the giant challenge before him or her in advancing in yoga. Here Patanjali gives a short list of our challenges, contrasting us from the Lord, who has no such challenges.

In the path of yoga, there are heaps of trouble of all kinds for the aspiring yogi. From an agitated mind to bodily pains, there is seemingly no end to the troubles faced by the practitioner. But the Lord, Patanjali declares, is unique in having no troubles.

Karma binds us to our material body and the world of illusion. To stop accumulating karma is the first goal of yoga, described as *karma-yoga*, which is why this is the first type of yoga presented in detail by Krishna in the *Bhagavad-gita*. But the Lord, Patanjali declares, is unique in having no karma.

Once we stop accumulating karma, we still have to deal with the mountains of "seed-karma," karma yet to fructify, the results of past karmic action. After describing *karma-yoga*, Krishna describes *jnana-yoga*, the yoga of knowledge and wisdom, as the technique for eliminating this kind of future karmic reaction. But the Lord, Patanjali declares, is unique in having no future results of karma.

Lastly, we are deeply influenced by our unconscious. Neuroscience teaches us that even the simplest decision, such as choosing between orange or apple juice, happens on an unconscious and even gut level beyond what we can perceive. Everything we do is influenced by unconscious forces, or, to use the language of the *Yoga Sutras*, by our *samskaras*, our subliminal registers. But the Lord, Patanjali declares, is unique in having no such unconscious influence.

A yogi should therefore understand that he or she never was, is not, and never will be God. Souls are many in number; God is unique. The soul is divine, but the soul is not God. We are one with God in one sense, but we are simultaneously different in another.

25. The Lord has unparalleled omniscience.

God, as the source of everything, is also the source of all knowledge, so naturally He knows everything.

He is also all-pervading. His infinite nature allows Him to be fully present in all places at the same time. By this, He can also know everything.

God is free of defects, so His perception is never mistaken, nor is His memory subject to failure. Because He is unlimited, His capacity to store and retrieve information is limitless.

Because God is unborn, primordial, and ever-existing, and never subject to troubles or karma, there was never a time when He was in illusion or limited in any sense, so His knowledge-acquiring abilities were never compromised.

Since God is in our heart, He has full knowledge of all the thoughts and desires we ever manifested, in this life and all others, thus knowing us better than we could ever hope to know ourselves.

And since the Lord has infinite intelligence and processing power, He can compile this information to reach an infinite number of conclusions about reality and can predict the future.

No matter how great a level of intuition and omniscience a yogi may hope to achieve, it will never be anything like that of the Lord. The soul and God are quite different in this regard.

26. Because He is unlimited by time, the Lord is the guru even of the ancients.

No one is equal to or superior to the Lord. All others, even the great teachers that have shaped history, are subservient to the guru of all gurus, the Lord. Not only is God the source of all knowledge, but His perfect existence is primordial.

27. The sacred syllable *om* represents Him.

The simplest sacred sound to represent the Lord is *om*. God also has innumerable holy names, such as Krishna, Rama, Narayana, and Vishnu in the yoga tradition and Yahveh and Allah in the Abrahamic traditions.

The names of God are as powerful as God Himself. In fact, there is no difference between God and His holy name. God's name has the power to cleanse your mistaken identification with matter and connect you with Him, just as being in His personal presence would. Thus, by chanting the name of God, you enter into direct communion with Him, according to the purity and focus of your chanting. This simple means of getting in touch with God brings great blessings and auspiciousness to your life.

The names invoke a more powerful connection to God, as they refer to one of God's specific personal forms, whereas the syllable *om* is more generic.

These sutras about the Lord demonstrate, among other things, that God is not to be understood as mere energy, source-energy, or light. To consider God to be only light is not accepted in any Indic school of thought, with the exception of the Shankara version of Vedanta, which is numerically smaller and has a less significant cultural impact than the Vaishnava Vedanta tradition. There are six schools of thought in the Indian spiritual tradition, and only one small part of one of them, the one proposed by Shankara, advocates the merging of the soul with God upon liberation.

Yet in the West, because yoga and Indian spirituality arrived with predominantly atheistic and Shankara-based conceptions, we find a predominance of the concept of God as energy. This is also due to the fact that those seeking these traditions in the West had often rejected their Christian or Muslim backgrounds, which had a personal conception of God.

To accept God as just energy, source-energy, or light is to sell yourself short. In *The 3T Path*, I explain the difference of the concepts of the personal and the impersonal. I also present arguments from the yoga tradition to explain the two concepts and the irrationalities of the energy-only concept of God.

Treating God only as energy is like finding your soulmate and using that person only to heat your feet at night, completely ignoring the person and using only the heat emanating from his or her body. It's like using the most incredible person you could ever hope to meet only to charge your cellphone, à la the movie *Matrix*, using their bio-electric energy but never speaking to them.

If you've taken the step of accepting the existence of something greater, don't stop at the concept of energy-only. Keep researching, use your brains, and practice the techniques necessary to attain the highest aspect of yoga, true *bhakti*.

28. Practice mantra meditation (*japa*) with this syllable, focusing your attention on the meaning of it.

Japa is Sanskrit for mantra meditation. Mantra meditation is to hold your focus on softly chanting a mantra. As in any meditation, the goal is to cease other thoughts or, at the very least, ignore other thoughts, bringing your attention to the object of meditation, which in this case is the *sound* of the mantra.

Japa is usually performed with meditation beads, which further help focus your mind.

Japa is the most traditional form of meditation. It's what I have been practicing since the mid-nineties and what I recommend to all my students. *Japa* is explicitly mentioned in both the *Yoga Sutras* and in the *Bhagavad-gita*, where Krishna says that it's the topmost form of *yajna*, an offering to and means of connecting with the divine.

The mantra used in *japa* should be carefully considered. Here Patanjali advocates the use of the simplest of all mantras, the syllable *om*, as a means of meditating on the Lord.

Use your critical intelligence in choosing a mantra. If your goal is to achieve loving union with the Lord, which is the goal of yoga, then you should use a mantra that contains the Lord's holy names or the syllable *om*, not the names of nature gods or other lesser deities. Then you should endeavor to understand to what aspect of God that name refers; that will direct your connection to God and determine the mood of your spirituality. Ganesha and Shiva are not the same. Shiva and Krishna are not the same being. Narayana and Krishna are not the same form of God. Each name refers to either a different being altogether or a different form of God. Don't accept mantras blindly. Find out more, study, and understand what you're doing. Patanjali here says, "Focus your attention on the meaning" of the mantra. Mantras are not all the same, and even different forms and names of God are not the same. There are important subtleties to be learned to fine-tune your spiritual practice and goals.

You won't be working your nature as an eternal soul if you choose mantras that have no transcendental element, such as mantras from Buddhist traditions that do not subscribe to the concept of a spiritual reality, the eternal soul, or God. You may pacify your mind, help your body, and become a better person – but you won't be advancing in yoga as presented in the *Yoga Sutras* or the *Bhagavad-gita*.

And you'll make no spiritual progress at all with the modern notion of chanting positive affirmations or power words, such as "I am strong" or "I am beautiful," and calling them a mantra. I'm not claiming that such phrases cannot be positive or useful or that they must be avoided, just that they will not bring about the same results as chanting mantras that directly connect you to God. If you want to use this technique to help you change your mindset, I would recommend that you also set aside time for a deeply spiritual *japa* practice. Solving a problem is good, but eradicating the root of all problems is best.

The mantra I use and recommend is the Hare Krishna mantra:

Hare Krishna, Hare Krishna
Krishna Krishna, Hare Hare
Hare Rama, Hare Rama
Rama Rama, Hare Hare

This is also known as the *maha-mantra*, which means the "great" mantra. It is widely recognized as the most powerful of all mantras in the yoga tradition. The first word, Hare, is an invocation to Radha, the feminine aspect of God. Krishna is a name of God meaning "the all-attractive." And Rama, another holy name, means "the source of bliss." These are the three sacred sounds of the *maha-mantra*. *Bhakti-yoga* masters explain that the *maha-mantra* is a powerful means to establish a connection with God in the mood of attaining loving service and divine protection. This mantra connects you with the sweetness and intimacy of God as Krishna, the speaker of the *Bhagavad-gita* and the master of all masters of yoga.

29. This practice results in self-realization and overcomes all obstacles.

Here Patanjali is referring to the general principle of submitting to the Lord, though one could also claim he is referring to the process of *japa*. They are, actually, one and the same, since God-focused *japa* is one of the principle means of taking shelter of the Lord.

The point is clear: devotion to God, or *bhakti*, is an all-powerful technique that grants perfection and self-realization and also removes all obstacles in your spiritual path.

Bhakti is thus both the means and the goal. It's the means for attaining perfection and the final goal of union in love with the Lord. This is why it's so effective.

30. The obstacles are those things that distract the mind, and they are as follows: disease, lack of interest, doubt, carelessness, lack of detachment, laziness, a mistaken view of life, not achieving a firm base, and lack of stability.

This is a list of temporary situations that prevent the yogi from maintaining his or her calm steady focus (*samadhi*).

Staying healthy is one of the important lifestyle choices for a yogi. An unhealthy body creates an unhealthy mind. Aches, pains, and illness do not go well with meditation. For those on the path of meditation-only yoga, these are real show-stoppers. For those on the path of an enlightened life, they are further challenges to overcome, with lessons to be learned in detachment and tolerance. But in either case, cultivating the best possible state of health is important on the path of yoga.

Apathy, lack of interest, and laziness means we cannot take our practice seriously. In such a state, we won't direct the time and energy to maintain our mental state of yoga.

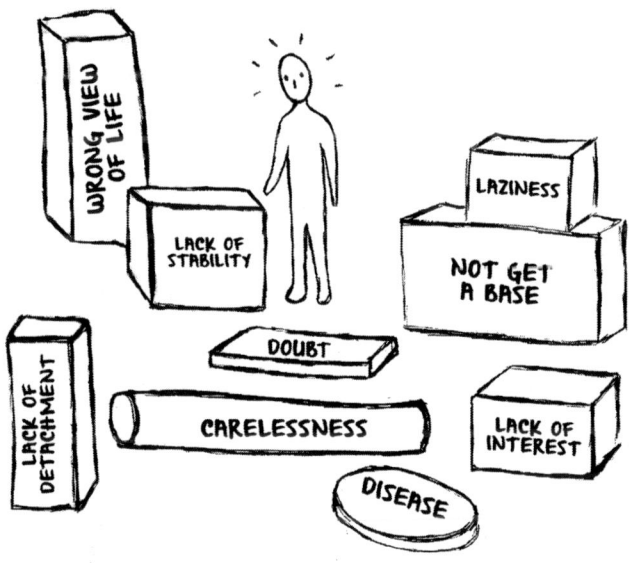

This apathy or laziness is usually caused by doubt, lack of detachment, or a mistaken view of life. When we lack the proper information about our nature, life, and what's good for us, there will be doubt as to what to do with ourselves. When we have doubt, we lack purpose and determination. In this state, we will usually become attached to things or situations we currently have in our grasp and thus will not have the power to leave our zone of comfort and attain new and higher states of consciousness.

With our minds thus lacking clarity, we lose our resolve. We have no stability, because we have no delineated path or fixed goal. When we lose our purpose, we default to superficiality and meaningless activity.

As explained earlier, yoga works on many fronts. From taking care of your health, to studying yoga wisdom, to working on your *bhakti*—everything is connected. Failure in one area will lessen the quality of your practice and have a negative influence on your ability to perform in the other areas.

31. These obstacles are accompanied by the following: suffering, depression, bodily trembling, and unbalanced breathing.

We all wish to avoid suffering. You could say that the very reason to take on yoga (or, for that matter, any path of liberation) is to become forever free of suffering. There is no way to become free of suffering while still embodied, or, more precisely, while we still identify with the body. Thus, suffering is here placed at the top of the list of what happens when we face obstacles in attaining the perfection of yoga.

Depression and melancholy arise when we fantasize about the future or think about the past. By cultivating mundane desires, or to use the more scientific term, extrinsic goals, we set ourselves up for unhappiness. First, if we desire something in the future, then automatically we are unhappy to not have it yet. Second, if our desire is frustrated, we naturally become despondent. And third, even if our extrinsic goal is achieved, we still feel a tinge of sadness as the positive feeling dissipates and we cannot escape the realization that whatever it was we achieved was temporary and limited. If we cannot avoid altogether this mindset, which I call the Fantasy Paradigm, we are doomed to unhappiness and frustration.

Bodily trembling and unbalanced breathing are physiological disturbances that would affect the meditation-only yogi but not the enlightened-life yogi. Having said that, it should always be a priority for the yogi to optimize his or her physical well-being.

32. The practice of "one-truth" will ward off these problems.

Since this verse ends the section on *Iswara*, the Lord, we can conclude that the one categorical aspect of reality (*tattva*, truth) being mentioned here is that of God as the source of all other truths or, to use a philosophical term, "the absolute truth."

In Indic philosophy, there are three *tattvas*, fundamental categories of existence, or truths. Think of them as three boxes in which you can put everything that exists. One *tattva* is of material energy. Everything material, every real, physical "thing" in the universe, falls into this category. Another *tattva* contains the innumerable individual souls—all of us, whether we happen to be stuck in a material body or liberated. And lastly, there is the *tattva* of God. In this box, there is only one item: the Lord. By suggesting the "practice of this one truth," Patanjali is repeating the instruction that started this section: "Practice devotion to the Lord and you will attain perfection."

To summarize the theological section of the *Yoga Sutras*, we can state with full conviction that regardless of the path chosen, be it the path of meditation only or the path of enlightened life, the yogi must ultimately focus his or her full attention on *bhakti*, devotion to the Lord. *Bhakti* is the highest and final state of yoga, as confirmed both by Patanjali and the *Bhagavad-gita*.

The yogi who chooses to disregard God and the practice of *bhakti* is in for a very long ride and will fail to achieve success until such a time as he or she places *bhakti* in its rightful place, as the most elevated yogic practice and the ultimate spiritual goal.

33. Mental clarity will come to those who 1) are friendly toward those who are happy, 2) show compassion to those who are suffering, 3) experience joy in regards to piety, and 4) neglect impiety.

In this section, Patanjali raises the topic of mental clarity, which is a state of mind necessary for yoga.

In our day-to-day lives, we will seldom experience deep, intense meditation, but we should seek to live in a state of mental clarity. This means having the vision to know what is good for you and what is not, what is to be done, what is to be avoided, and generally to have a lucid mental map. This mental map should show you both spiritual and material dimensions of life, reveal God and the presence of God in everything and everyone, and highlight the importance of seeking the well-being of others. Without mental clarity, we doom ourselves to endless blunders and frustration.

The recipe for mental clarity presented in this sutra is simple enough. First, we should appreciate and approach those who already have mental clarity, classified here as "the happy." We should seek their association by any means necessary – in the form of personal contact, books, video channels, mailing lists, and social media. The more you appreciate and emulate the qualities of the happy, the happier you'll become.

Second, we should practice compassion, which here is in the sense of helping others live better. As you experience your spiritual awakening, remember those who are still asleep, missing out on life. As you progress, help those who are behind you. Do this without pride, and you'll benefit yourself in the process.

Last, take an active stance in living piously. Commit and work toward being pious, truthful, and kind; doing the right thing; and living your dharma. At the same time, Patanjali warns, remain indifferent to impiety. Don't judge, don't be preachy, and don't consider yourself superior to others. Don't look for faults in others' behavior. Here's a simple rule to avoid becoming a nuisance: give advice only to those who either request it or are under your care. Let the laws of physics and the laws of the land limit what others do. It's not your concern. Focus on yourself. Plenty to work on and improve right there, I guarantee you.

34. Or, it is achieved by breathing exercises.

Neuroscience has confirmed the influence that breathing techniques have on the brain. There are many techniques, which vary the time for intake, retention, and exhalation. Basically, though, simple deep breaths are the ticket. Slow, deep breathing, studies show, calms the mind. More importantly, once your amygdala, your animal brain, kicks in, breathing is practically the *only* thing that will calm you down. Panic, anger, fear, accelerated heart rate, and increased blood pressure are all symptoms of your amygdala in full swing, which can be pacified by slow, deep breaths. Throughout the day, try to become aware of your breathing, and when you do, treat yourself to slow, deep breaths and watch your brain mellow and sharpen at the same time—it's mental clarity kicking in.

35. Or, it is achieved by meditating on a sense object.

This sutra describes a common mindfulness technique. Mindfulness, too, has been confirmed by neuroscience as a powerful tool for increasing mental focus and peace. The practice is to place your full attention on any given sense object and hold your attention there as long and well as you can. Even a few minutes of this practice will benefit you. Your mind stops flying through time and space, the incessant inner chatter is silenced, and the beautiful light of consciousness can shine through. The more you practice, the better you'll get, and the higher the quality of your life will be.

36. Or, it is achieved by maintaining an enlightened, painless state of mind.

As the mind becomes pacified by the different yoga practices and lifestyle choices, our nature shines through. The soul's natural state of being is light and joy. After all, if you're not your body but an eternal spiritual being, what is the difficulty? What is there to bring you down? The answer is nothing but your own mistaken view of reality—illusion. The fifth-century commentator of the *Yoga Sutras*, Vyasa, says that we should act with our intelligence focused on our heart *chakra*. A modern interpretation of that instruction would be to act in love. Let love guide your actions and words. Let love pervade your plans and worldview. You've experienced this before: when you act out of love, you naturally feel enlightened and painless. The effort to maintain that high state of consciousness is yoga in practice.

37. Or, it is achieved when the mind is free of future desire.

This is a key concept; there is no getting around it. If you hanker for future results, yearning for the pleasure some future thing or event will supposedly bring you, you've fallen off the yoga wagon. To the degree that you're cultivating that mindset, you'll experience a combination of anxiety, stress, fear, envy, frustration, and a host of other unpleasant emotions. In the language of the 3T Path, this is the Fantasy Paradigm, which I urge you to avoid.

When you feel this happening, stop it. Don't be drawn in by the rush of affective forecasting, the body's drug-induced sensation we experience when dreaming of future pleasure. The buzz we get with affective forecasting is not too different from a drug high; it feels nice enough while you're on it, but the sensation quickly passes and you're left worse off than before, frustrated and unhappy with reality, looking for the next high. Meanwhile, you're doing a poor job of living life as it is; you're missing out on life. Take deep breaths and draw your mind back to the here and now, to your dharma at hand. Regain your harmony with reality and you'll again experience the peace and well-being of a steady mind.

38. Or, it is achieved when the mind has knowledge attained from dreams and sleep.

The experience of sleep is often used in sacred yoga literature to help us better understand and deal with our mundane reality and the ultimate transcendental reality beyond it.

In this regard, it's important to better understand the three levels of reality we can experience: the dream world, the material world, and the transcendental realm of the Divine.

Practically every night, you enter another level of reality—a dream world. That world is not made of the same stuff as the material world. The water in your dreams is not H2O; it's made of something else. Your body in your dreams doesn't have any actual cells. And yet you still experience individual personhood, a variety of forms and colors, interactions with other people and things, and different sensations. And while you're dreaming, you believe in it; it is your reality, life as you know it, as long as the dream lasts. Then you wake up.

When you wake up, you become aware that what had seemed real was actually just a dream. You are now in the material world. Naturally, you conclude that this waking reality is the "real" thing.

But yoga is calling you to wake up once more, this time from the material world, and perceive that there is a third level of reality: the transcendental realm. That, the sacred texts claim, is the ultimate and only truly real world. This reality is beyond *samsara*, achieved through the portal of *samadhi* and reached by the practice of yoga.

39. Or, it is achieved by meditating on anything you prefer.

As science now confirms, the act of meditation pacifies the mind, regardless of what one chooses as the object of meditation. It means simply to focus the mind on any one thing, be it as transcendental as the sound of God's holy name or as mundane as a dot on the wall. The act of stilling the endless mental chatter and experiencing consciousness as purely as possible is in itself beneficial.

There is, however, one distinction: As Patanjali points out here, you can achieve all the physiological benefits of meditation by focusing your mind on any one point, no matter what it is, but you can only achieve spiritual benefit, in the truest sense of the word, when the focus is spiritual. One can focus on the syllable *om*, the Hare Krishna *maha-mantra*, or directly on God Himself, visualizing Him in the heart, as *Paramatma*, as recommended in the *Bhagavad-gita*, the *Yoga Sutras*, and many other sacred texts. When you choose a transcendental focus for your meditation, you have everything to gain and nothing to lose. You'll get the same mental and physical benefits but with the added bonus of spiritual awakening.

40. The yogi has mastery from the smallest particle to the totality of matter.

Once the mind is perfectly pacified in yoga, the yogi has nothing more to fear. He has attained mastery over all material existence, as he or she is no longer dependent on it. No combination of external events can disturb the accomplished yogi, not even the destruction of his or her physical body.

In this regard, there is an amusing story about Alexander the Great and a yogi. It is said that Alexander the Great came to this yogi in a forest after having already conquered so many lands, desiring to take a yogi back to Macedonia with him. The yogi refused his request, which made Alexander fly into a fit of rage. He threatened to kill the yogi, bragging that he was the great king Alexander. The yogi said he had no fear of death, as he could not die; only his body could be destroyed. The yogi then looked into Alexander's eyes and said, "You are no king. You are a slave of my slave!" Astonished at the yogi's words, Alexander asked him to explain himself. The yogi, replied, "I have fully conquered anger, and so anger is my slave. But you so easily gave in to anger, so you are a slave to anger. Thus, you are a slave to my slave."

Too bad the yogi didn't go back with Alexander. Can you imagine how great it would have been for spiritual yoga to be taught in ancient Greece? That could have changed the course of history.

41. *Samapatti* is complete absorption in meditation. This happens when the influence of the fluctuations of the mind weaken. In this state, the mind becomes like a transparent jewel that is colored by whatever it focuses on, be it the seer, the instrument of seeing, or the seen.

Samapatti is total focus on anything, including the self that is doing the meditation, the sense organ being used to perceive the object in question, or the thing itself. These teachings on *samapatti* will reveal to us the different levels of super-intense focus and meditation. They are, practically speaking, unattainable for anyone not following the path of meditation-only yoga for decades on end, but nonetheless give us a glimpse of the power of the highly trained human mind.

42. The first stage is known as *savitarka-samapatti*: meditation mixed with physical awareness, with notions of the word used to describe the object, its meaning, and previous knowledge regarding it.

In stage one, the meditator cannot focus exclusively on the object of meditation. The word associated with the object pops into his or her awareness, and so too do the meaning of the word and all knowledge associated with the object. The concept is that the meditation is clouded by the presence and influence of this previously acquired information.

43. The second stage is known as nirvitarka-samapatti: meditation without past impressions, with no use of memory; the object of meditation now shines forth in the mind alone.

In stage two, the object of meditation exists on its own in the mind of the meditator. No words or previously accumulated thoughts corresponding to the object arise.

44. The third and fourth stages are known as *savichara* and *nirvichara samapatti* and can be explained in the same way, with the focus now being the subtle nature of the object of meditation.

Stages three and four are like one and two in the sense of having the use of words, meanings, and past experiences concerning the object and then not having these.

But now the focus is so deep that the meditator is perceiving not the object itself, but the underlying nature of the object.

For example, if a yogi is meditating on a stone, his or her focus will no longer be on the stone itself, but on the mineral components of the stone, then the molecules of the stone, and finally the subatomic energy component of the stone.

Don't be discouraged. These people were not doing anything else for decades on end. Comparing these masters of supernatural states of mind with one of us is worse than comparing an Olympian gold medalist with a couch potato. Remember, it's an entirely different path of yoga they were following. You can excel in the one that is recommended and achievable to all of us, the path of living an enlightened life, as described in *The 3T Path*.

45. The subtle nature of an object leaves no visible mark.

As the yogi goes deeper and deeper in his or her meditation, he or she penetrates beyond the energy aspect of reality and perceives the underlying causes of reality itself. This is like the idea of the "realm of forms" put forth by Plato, in which the concept of a horse, the ideal horse, exists beyond all real horses running about. In yoga, the ultimate and most subtle state of matter is called *ahankara*.

What's the fun in doing that? you may ask. Well, the idea is that as you progress in this form of meditation, you experience increasingly purer states of *sattva*, which naturally fill the yogi with great joy.

According to Indic philosophy, *sattva* is the highest of the three vibrations, or strings, that form matter as a whole. From these three, all other forms of matter and material energy arise.

Interestingly, completely pure *sattva* is equivalent to spiritual, transcendental energy, the source of perfect bliss for the soul.

So, with the use of any object in matter, the yogi can use his or her laser-like focus to peel away the object's increasingly subtle layers of physical reality, toward an ever-purer perception of *sattva*. He or she can distill the essence of reality with the power of meditation and with that, experience higher and higher levels of the peaceful bliss associated with *sattva*.

This isn't so farfetched. You've probably experienced a taste of this blissful peace with even a beginner's level of practice of meditation or mindfulness. Without being aware of the intricacies involved, I suspect that everyone has experienced the joy of a peaceful moment, of a calm mind. The yogis being described here are doing something similar, but on a much grander scale. They experience bliss for hours on end, compared to our few moments.

46. These forms of *samapatti* are *samadhi* with seed.

"Seed" here refers to matter. Even advanced yogis with such awesome abilities as described above were ever so slightly involved in mundane consciousness, as seen by the fact that the focus of their meditation was an object of the material world. The word *seed* implies that such an advanced yogi still has the potential to get tangled up in bodily life and fall from his or her state of cosmic peace and joy. These yogis in the state of *sabija samadhi*, or *samadhi* with seed, are not out of the woods yet. Like shipwreck victims who have managed to miraculously swim and float for untold miles but are still not quite out of the water, they can still be dragged back to the ocean of birth and death.

47. The bliss of the inner self arises in perfect mental clarity.

This is the holy grail of yoga. Beyond any process of mundane thought, in perfect mental clarity, the yogi experiences the soul and the grace of spiritual bliss. No longer is the yogi just blissing out on peace in the rarefied subtle realm of matter. Now the yogi has transcended matter and experiences spiritual reality.

48. In this state, wisdom conveys the underlying principles of existence.

This perfect state of consciousness uncovers the core truth of reality. The yogi is gifted with all-powerful wisdom capable of revealing the essence of all there is. No more wrong-turns and no more illusion. All is clear. All is perfect.

49. This perfect state of *samadhi* has a different focus from that of reason and scriptural study because of its unique characteristic.

Yoga requires the use of all three sources of knowledge: 1) authority, 2) reason, and 3) direct perception. Ultimately, having learned all there is to learn from scripture and guru, having fully thought things through with reason, one is left to experience higher and higher levels of consciousness directly. Book knowledge and reason will guide you in the right direction, but ultimate spiritual reality and love are to be experienced directly.

50. The mental impressions created in this state of wisdom obstruct mundane impressions.

Spiritual experience replaces material experience. Theocentric loving spiritual life takes over from needy egocentric material life. In the *Bhagavad-gita* Krishna describes spiritual experience as being "a higher taste." This higher taste of spiritual existence, truth, and wisdom defeat lower mundane thought. Scriptural knowledge, the words of the guru, and reason are all very good. But it's not until you've tasted the bliss of spiritual existence for yourself that you'll truly be convinced.

51. When even this ceases, everything ceases, and the ultimate state of seedless *samadhi* is achieved.

The final goal is achieved after carefully and gradually cultivating more and more direct spiritual experience. A time comes when the yogi has finished the process of obstructing all mundane, selfish, and illusory impressions, and exclusively experiences spiritual bliss and perfect, unobstructed spiritual vision. In *bhakti* terms, the yogi is now constantly 100 percent focused on God. With undeviating attention, the yogi is always connected with him- or herself and with the higher self, God, and sees God in everything and everyone. At this point, there is no danger of falling down. The yogi has achieved liberation from all material existence, forever.

SADHANA-PADA

1. Yoga in action consists of noble behavior, study, and devotion to God.

Here we find the classic threefold path of yoga—three avenues to pursue to elevate your consciousness and consequently reduce suffering.

"Noble behavior" is a translation of the word *tapa*. It's about the choices you make in life and how you live. It's about choosing not what's immediately more satisfying to your senses or pride, but what's best in the long run for your deeper self. This is a determining factor in making your life better. Self-responsibility: you must assume full responsibility for the quality of your life. From diet to sex, from who you hang out with to what habits you have, you have to take the long view, with your enduring well-being as the guide to all your choices.

Next we have *svadhyaya*, which refers to study that will guide your self-improvement and self-realization. To make the right decisions, you need knowledge. Information is power, and the more information you have on life and the workings of your mind, the more power you'll have to attain peace and joy. This means knowledge on two levels: the practical and the metaphysical – knowledge to help you deal with this world and knowledge to shape your spiritual path. I use the word *wisdom* in this regard to emphasize that this is the kind of knowledge that will positively change how you react to and deal with life.

Last, there is *isvara-pranidhana* (devotion). Devotion to God is the most powerful practice in yoga. It's the key to success and the object of success at the same time – the means *and* the end. Because of this, it's also the most difficult to access and, once activated, the most difficult to use with intelligence.

We see that many people can't even approach devotion in the first place, having developed, like I once did, a distaste for the whole topic. Many otherwise-intelligent people dislike devotion to God because of the less-than-ideal behavior of many who not only openly express their devotion to God, but whose worst traits are fueled by that devotion. Devotion gives power. But power in the wrong hands produces pain.

It is my hope that the peaceful, inclusive, and intelligent presentation of spirituality in this ancient path will gradually replace the uncivilized expressions of devotion to God we see today—and the oppression, hatred and violence they manifest.

These three practices are mutually helpful. Advancing in one helps you better practice the other.

Here's a graphic presentation I use in *The 3T Path*:

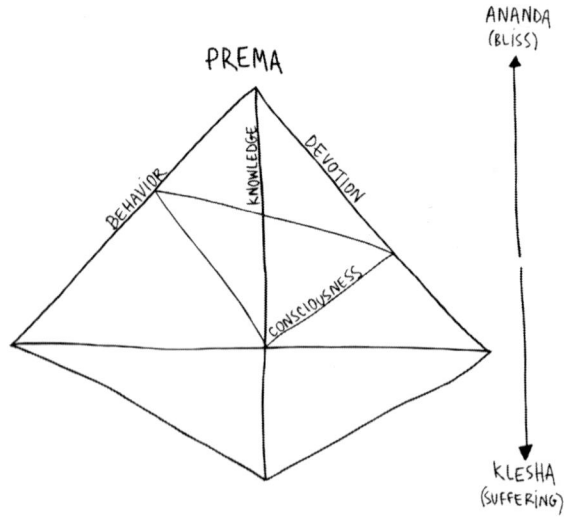

Your state of consciousness is represented by a triangle in the middle. The triangle is formed by the degree of advancement in each of the three avenues. The higher the state of consciousness, the better you feel. Practically speaking, happiness is the gauge of advancement. The more you work on yourself, the more you experience bliss—*ananda*. The more disturbed and dark your consciousness, the more you experience pain—*klesha*.

Samadhi is the perfection achieved when you master all three. Here the word used is *prema*: pure spiritual love, the final and most perfect state of existence.

2. Its purpose is to bring about *samadhi* and reduce pain.

All our pain is self-imposed. Even physical pain is processed by the mind; if the mind is shut down, the pain ceases to exist. Our daily anxieties, fears, and other negative emotions causing us pain are entirely virtual. Such pain exists only because we set ourselves up to experience it and then allow our minds to dwell on it. As we progress in yoga, we learn to process life in increasingly more intelligent and less painful ways.

Few people understand that spirituality means having a better life right here and now. We tend to associate where we live, our marital status, our careers, and the things we own with the quality of our life. We think, therefore, that to have a better life, it will be necessary to change all these things. And that to have a spiritual life will imply not having a career, family, or things. But that's not it at all. We principally have to change our minds, because that's where the problem lies.

3. This pain manifests in the form of ignorance, misconception of the nature of the self, fantasizing about the future, aversion, and fear of death.

4. From ignorance comes all other forms of pain, whether dormant, weak, sporadic, or fully manifest.

This is a key point of Eastern spirituality: all suffering is born of ignorance. The concept is simple: if you know how to live, you'll be happy. If you don't, you'll make mistakes and suffer. If you walk around in the dark, you're bound to walk into furniture or a wall, or trip over something. This is quite different from the Abrahamic concept of good versus evil. This brings the fight to you. It's you only. You are your only enemy. Take the trouble to learn, put that into practice, and you're home free.

5. Ignorance means to consider the non-permanent as permanent, the impure as pure, unhappiness as happiness, and the non-self as the self.

The nature of the soul is pure, joyful, and permanent. This is who we really are. We are eternally existing beings of pure heart and unlimited happiness. That's the good news.

The bad news is that, at this moment, due to our ignorance, we're a bit confused. We're not sure who we are. We think we're the material body, something clearly not permanent.

Because we're attached to this body, our hearts cannot be pure. We identify with the demands of the body, physical limitations, and a win-lose mentality born out of competition and survival. In the metaphysical, spiritual plane, there is no scarcity. The more love you give, the more you get. The more just you are, the more justice there is. But in the material dimension, if you give away an inch, you've got one inch less. If you share a bowl of rice, it's one bowl less you're going to get. The more we identify with matter, the meaner we become.

As our hearts become impure with selfishness, we become unhappy. It's a curious, but inescapable fact of life: the more you concern yourself with your own needs, the more miserable you become.

As we blow away the fog of confusion, starting with some deep thought about who we really are, we change the way we go about life and naturally become increasingly joyous.

6. One misconception about the nature of the self is to consider the eye and the power of seeing to be the same.

Patanjali poetically describes our misidentification with the physical body by giving the example of the eye and the power of seeing.

The eye is made of matter. It's a physical thing. The eye does not actually see. Seeing is an act of life. Dead things don't see. Life is a symptom of the soul. The power of seeing pertains to the eternal metaphysical self.

In short, don't confuse the I with the eye.

7. Fantasizing about the future is born of attachment to superficial pleasure.

Once you misunderstand who you are, you'll mistake what will make you happy. Despite crushing evidence from our own lives and research in the field of psychology, economics, history, and sociology, we persist as a society in the greatest error: pursuing happiness from the outside-in and in the future.

Life is not about what you have; it's about how you live it. And the worst way to live your life is by focusing on the what, especially when that is something in the future. Even if you have the business you desire, the car you wished for, the dream house you planned, and six-pack abs to show off, none of this will make you happy. Things don't make you happy. It's what you do with your things, how you live your life, right here and now, that makes you happy or not. So much so, that in the end you could be riding the bus, living in a one-bedroom apartment, and have a "dad bod" and still be happier and more realized than the folks in the Hamptons, Saudi princes, and the jet-set crowd. I call this "cartoon wisdom", because it's so obvious even children's cartoons explain this.

Chasing after desires and fantasizing about the future is guaranteed to bring you varying levels of anxiety, low self-worth, fear, and envy. To some degree, it will leave you frustrated and confused.

We persist in this painful attachment to mundane, superficial pleasure, not knowing there is a better option, a better way to live our lives: focusing on our *dharma* in the here and now, in divine connection.

8. Aversion is born of suffering.

Once the mind is on the surface of life, we'll naturally develop a see-saw of attachment and aversion, *raga* and *dvesa*. You either want something to happen or you want something to NOT happen. As we live life in this way, there is no peace. Instead, we experience hankering and anxiety. There is the added problem that something we're attached to may later become something we are averse to, or the other way around. Anybody who has married and divorced can understand this principle.

9. Fear of death affects even the wise. It is deeply rooted.

It takes a tremendous amount of spiritual advancement, or an incredible focus on duty, to not fear death. It's almost like we're hardwired to fear death. Yet, death will come, and we better be prepared for it. It's trite, but it can't be said enough: the only thing certain in life is death. Yours and everybody else's.

It's healthy to contemplate the impermanent nature of our bodies. Never take for granted how much time you or your loved ones have left in this incarnation.

Prepare yourself for death today, because today may be your last. Be clear about your spiritual identity and your post-death destination.

I also recommend that you keep not only your affairs in order, but also, especially, your relationships. Let everybody in your inner circle know you love them and work out any misunderstandings as soon as possible. Just ask yourself, "What if I had to go now?" Any regrets? Anything you'd beg another day, week or month to take care of? Then do it now.

10. All these forms of pain are subtle and cease to exist when the self returns to its original state.

The good news is that pain is an illusion that affects the materially embodied. When one has attained liberation from matter, by yoga, all one's pains are permanently destroyed.

The nature of pure existence is pure bliss.

11. Meditation eliminates these painful states of mind.

The more we meditate on the nature of our suffering and their roots, the more we can change our way of life to avoid hurting ourselves. We alone are the agents of all our suffering. Thus, we have the power to stop it.

12. These pains are at the root of our karma and are experienced in this life and in future lives.

All involvement with matter is driven by these five pains, starting with ignorance and misidentification with the material body. Our entire existence in the material world and in the cycle of birth and death is caused by our minds being afflicted with these mistakes.

This, in turn, places us under the Law of Karma, where the *dharmic* degree of each action determines the material quality of the reaction we'll have to experience. The more attuned you are with your *dharma*, the better your karma.

But karma is karma. Sure, better to have it good than bad, but that's like saying it's better to be under house arrest with an ankle bracelet than in jail. For the soul, karma is always an endless source of misery.

The sub-goal of yoga, therefore, is to become free of karma.

13. So long as the root exists, it ripens as a type of birth, a set duration of life, and a certain life experience.

So long as a soul has karma, it is forced to remain in the material world to experience it. For that it needs a material body, be it a luminous subtle celestial body or the body of an insect or aquatic on Earth. Each body comes with a pre-determined duration of life and a whole set of experiences and situations that the soul must undergo to learn from its past mistakes or benefit from its past good deeds.

It's worthy of note that though a certain type of life may be predetermined by previously accumulated karma, the quality of your life experience is entirely up to you.

You may be living out the good karma of fame, wealth, and beauty but live in constant anxiety, fear, and hankering. Or you may have a whole series of challenges such as low income, physical disabilities, and a bad government but learn to take those in your stride and live a happy life.

The power to live well does not depend on your karma, but rather in how you choose to experience life.

14. These results are caused by good and bad deeds, and their fruits are pleasure and pain.

Good deeds are actions according to *dharma*. Bad deeds are actions opposed to *dharma*. One generates good karma, the other bad karma. Good karma creates pleasant situations, and bad karma creates difficult situations.

It's too late now for you to change the karma you have due to you in this life. But here is what you can do:

1. Maximize your good karma by following your *dharma* nicely and honoring every good thing that happens to you by doing your best in response to it.
2. Minimize your bad karma by using adversity to grow as a person and to become detached from material life.
3. Improve more and more the quality of your life by adjusting your mind and applying the techniques laid out in this book and in *The 3T Path*.

4. Take your self-realization in yoga seriously and free yourself of all karma in this lifetime so that you'll never have to take birth again.

In this way, you can have a great life now and become liberated when your time's up.

15. One who has had a spiritual awakening can understand that there is only misery in this world, due to karmic reactions, pain, past impressions, and mental agitation.

A fish out of water can never be happy. And right now, we are fish out of water. We are brilliant eternal individuals trapped in a world made of lifeless matter. We are under the strict control of the laws of nature, bound by time. From birth to death, we suffer pain in endless forms. Past impressions linger in our minds, twisting our current behavior and providing even more suffering. And to top it all, our minds are always agitated, fluctuating non-stop, giving us no peace.

Seeking enlightenment is the only smart move. And the good news is that on the path of enlightenment comes the diminution of all these above-cited troubles and an increase in peace and joy. Life gets better at every step on the yoga ladder.

16. Avoid the suffering that is yet to come.

This is the compassionate advice from all on the spiritual path: you need not suffer endlessly. Act now and the misery can end.

17. Confusing the seer with the seen is the source of all suffering.

The seer is the soul. The seen is matter. Two totally different energies. A basic point emphasized in yoga is to understand the existence of the two and know how to differentiate between them. We, living souls, need to extricate ourselves from dead, lifeless matter.

18. What can be seen is illumination, activity, and inertia, which form the senses and all of material creation. These exist for one of two purposes: to provide spiritual liberation or to provide material enjoyment.

This is a quick summary of how yoga sees the material world around us. Underlying all matter are the three vibrations, or strings, known as the *gunas*, briefly mentioned in the comment of Sutra 1.45. There, *sattva* was presented as being the purest form of matter; here it

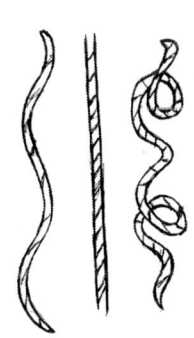

is referred to as "illumination." *Rajas* is referred to here as "activity." *Rajas* leads to the disturbance of the other modes, the agitation that brings about change. And *tamas* is referred to here as "inertia." It's darkness and stagnation. In the books *The 3T Path* and *A Comprehensive Guide to the Bhagavad-gita* you'll find a more detailed explanation of the *gunas*.

These three *gunas* are the building blocks of all material reality. Like the three primary colors that are used to create all colors, from these three, all manifestations of matter and material experience are created. This is the seen.

And the seer, the soul, can use this energy for one of two purposes: 1) to foolishly seek out material enjoyment or 2) to wisely seek spiritual liberation.

Seeking out material enjoyment just doesn't work. I've tried it. You've tried. We've all tried this over and over again, for countless millennia. Our minds just get agitated and we get anxious, hurt and frustrated. Then we die.

Plan B is to sit down and think things out a bit. Try to find out what's going on and why no one can get satisfaction. Figure out who and where we really are. Then you'll get your "aha" moment and your spiritual quest will begin. From that point on, you'll still use material energy, the *gunas*, but for a nobler and wiser purpose: to get away from them. Just as vaccines are made using the disease-causing virus or bacteria, so too will you create the solution to the *guna*-disease (material existence) using the *gunas*. And as a bonus part of the treatment, you live an increasingly better, more joyful, and more peaceful life. A win-win situation.

19. Material energy can be categorized as specific, nonspecific, marked, and unmarked.

This *sutra* refers to the complex metaphysics of Indic philosophy, specifically of Sankhya. You can't see the *gunas*, but from them arise things you can see and touch. In this way, the sages of Sankhya classified reality in different levels, from the most subtle, referred to as the unmarked in this sutra, to the most visible, the "specific."

20. The seer is the power to see. Although pure, the soul can see the images of the mind.

How do the seer and the seen interact? Through the mind. The soul is not interacting with material energy. Only our body and mind are interacting with the world around us. And we are only witnessing this through images in our mind.

21. Material energy exists only for the sake of the soul.

Material reality's only purpose is to serve the souls in their pursuit of either material experience or liberation. In theistic terms, God created this world for us. Not us humans on this Earth. But "us" as in all the living beings of all species in all corners of this and other universes. Matter has no consciousness; thus it has no purpose onto itself.

22. Though material energy ceases to exist for a liberated yogi, it continues to exist for other souls still trapped in the material world.

Though a prisoner may have served his or her time and be set free, the jail continues to exist for other inmates.

23. When the seer and the seen come together, the nature and power of both are revealed.

The soul can understand its nature and power in comparison to dead matter. And the nature and power of material energy can only by perceived by the soul.

24. They come together because of ignorance.

Why are we here? Yoga is adamant in stating that ignorance leads to all other suffering. But not so much is said about how it all began. Why did I become ignorant? When? How?

If we are eternal living persons, then we are endowed with the divine quality of free will. It's nonsensical to speak of a person without free will; that would be a robot. Without free will, there cannot be love. Love is meaningless if it's not optional. For there to be the option of loving, there must also exist the option of not loving.

No sane person would want to be surrounded by robots instead of real people. Imagine having a spouse and children, all just programmable robots, doing everything you want. That would be creepy.

God is no creep. A thousand years ago, Anselm defined God as "that than which nothing greater can be thought." A non-creepy God is clearly greater than a creepy one.

So, assuming God is not a creep, it makes sense that He too would not like to be surrounded by sycophant robots. Like you, He would prefer to be surrounded by real loving people who are there because they choose to be, in mutual reciprocation and bliss. This is pretty much the generally accepted definition of God's abode in all theistic traditions, including yoga.

In that scenario, what would happen if a soul decides to *not* be there? There must be an alternative to make the choice of being there valid. What if I don't want to be around God? What if I have other plans? This would be reasonable, if unwise.

It is, therefore, necessary for there to be a reality in which the soul can live out its fantasies in varying degrees of forgetfulness of God.

God kindly provides for this with the creation of the material world. That's why we're here.

You stay only if you want to. And as soon as you change your mind, you can get out. While you're here, the Law of Karma means you get your due according to the way you're using your free will, which is perfectly fair. When you recover your sanity and understand that, by definition, God is the most attractive person in creation and that hanging around Him (and Her) is the greatest thing to do, you can do it. Krishna means "the all-attractive." Achieving *samadhi* is just snapping out of this weird idea that it would be better to forget God and live on your own in some self-centered fantasy, misidentifying the self as the body.

Once that is done, ignorance is quickly dissipated and you become liberated.

25. When ignorance is gone, matter and spirit come apart, awarding perfect freedom to the soul.

The Bible tells us that knowledge will set us free. Knowledge plays an essential role in yoga spirituality as well. The more you seek to

understand who you are, where you are, and what in the world is going on, the better your chances of living well. And as you dig really deep, you're bound to get spiritual and then devotional.

26. To let go of ignorance, it's necessary to always cultivate awareness of the distinction of spirit and matter: *viveka*.

To be successful in yoga, we must train our minds to focus on what's real and best for us. What's best for us is to keep our mind in the here and now, focused on doing our *dharma*. And what's real is that we are spirit souls distinct from matter, living away from our natural state of existence.

How do we do that? The simple answer is that we do it by doing it! Just bring your mind back to it every time it slips away. There's no shortcut. No magical trick or cosmic blessing will set you up for life. No three-month retreat or $3,000 seminar will give you this power. You must just keep trying, day in and day out. If your mind slips, you bring it back. Simple as that, and so difficult too.

27. This wisdom is developed in seven stages.

In the oldest known commentary on the *Yoga Sutras*, the sage known as Vyasa (which means "the editor") describes yoga wisdom's seven stages:

    1. Knowing the source of suffering.

2. Eradicating the source of suffering.
3. Understanding the difference between the eternal self and the intelligence.
4. Achieving *viveka*.
5. No longer requiring the use of reason or intelligence to practice *viveka*.
6. Becoming free of a material body.
7. Achieving your full spiritual existence.

28. By practicing yoga, the impurities are destroyed and the light of knowledge shines through, revealing *viveka*.

It's worthy of note that just before the famous verse on the eight limbs of yoga (*ashtanga-yoga*), Patanjali emphasizes the purpose of the practice of yoga, *viveka*, to explain the difference between soul and body, spirit and matter.

29. The eight limbs of yoga are *yama, niyama, asana, pranayama,* withdrawal, concentration, meditation, and *samadhi*.

I chose to keep the names of five of the eight limbs in the original Sanskrit, as these terms are not only central to yoga, but have also become relatively well-known and understood by modern yoga enthusiasts.

30. The *yamas* are nonviolence, truthfulness, not stealing, chastity, and non-possessiveness.

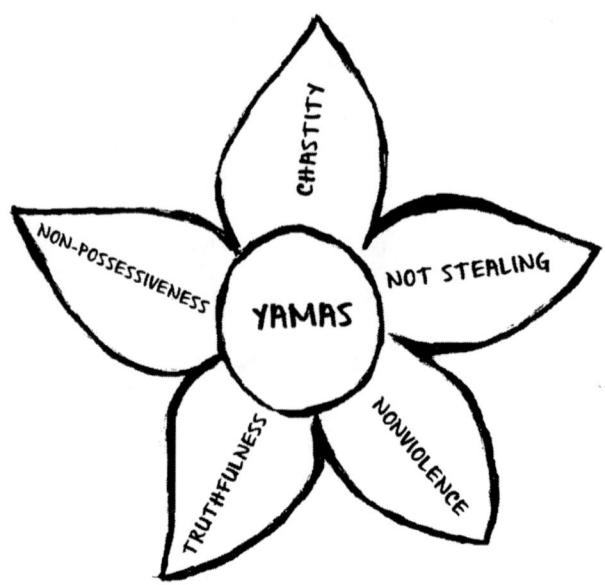

Detachment and decent behavior are the bases for advancement in life. There isn't much point in worrying about postures and breathing exercises, what to speak of meditation and devotion, if we can't first be decent human beings.

The mother of all codes of conduct is *ahimsa*: nonviolence. It is the supreme moral law that dictates all other moral observations. Nonviolence means never needlessly harming an innocent creature. This applies to all living beings, from humans to insects.

Ahimsa does not mean never using violence or causing harm. A common question posed by yoga students concerns Krishna, in the *Bhagavad-gita*, urging Arjuna to fight a bloody battle, made worse by the fact that Arjuna was fighting his own family members. Krishna set this up on purpose. He wanted to teach that in the execution of one's *dharma*, it's sometimes necessary to use violence. In the case of Arjuna, a warrior and general, there was no question. Violence was the expression of his duty. But *ahimsa* was not broken, because the violence was both needful and ethical. It was needful to reestablish the rightful government usurped by his evil cousin, Duryodhana. And it was ethical because all those present were professional soldiers willing to kill and die as part of their brutal but necessary *dharma*. The world always needs *dharmic* men and women willing to use force to combat and restrain those who use violence for selfish and evil ends.

For those of us who are not soldiers or involved in law enforcement, however, there is seldom a need for violence, save for the rare case of self-defense.

In practical terms, the biggest expression of *ahimsa* for yogis is to adopt a plant-based diet. Both as an expression of higher consciousness and because of it, killing innocent animals for the pleasure of one's tongue becomes intolerable. This is made worse by the realizations that killing animals for food is the principle cause of the ecological destruction of the planet and that eating meat is a major factor in some of the leading causes of death, such as heart disease and cancer.

Truthfulness is based on the simple principle that to attain truth, one must practice it. Lies and deception are a drain, even if in rare cases they might be necessary to execute one's *dharma*. How can you tell the difference? Simple: do the *ahimsa* test. Will lying and deceiving needlessly hurt an innocent person or animal? Then you must not do it. Will not lying or deceiving bring harm to an innocent person? Then lie and deceive you must.

Not stealing needs no explanation. But again, the *ahimsa* principle comes into play. Should you steal secrets or equipment from an evil doer in the hopes of defeating him? Yes, of course, if it is your *dharma*. But should you steal from innocent people for personal profit? Of course not.

Chastity means controlling your sex organs and using them only when appropriate. When is it appropriate? Opinions vary, but a blanket description is to restrict sex to a sacred union. And why is that? Because of *ahimsa*. Children born outside a sacred union often suffer the absence of their father, in some cases their mother, or both. Mothers left to raise children by themselves suffer more than those with loving partners to provide support. And society, statistics all over the world show, suffers with the anti-social behavior of single-parent children.

Non-possessiveness is a type of detachment. It means being aware that all you possess is on loan and not really yours. Anything you have can be taken away from you at a moment's notice and is in no way a part of you. If you have it, use it to further your *dharmas*. If you don't have it anymore, that's fine, too. It doesn't mean not to care or be grateful or to not take steps to safeguard your belongings. It just means not to identify with any possession to the point that you feel it defines who you are or that your happiness depends on having it.

31. These *yamas* are a great vow. They apply to everyone always. Occupation, time, place, and circumstance do not limit it.

Patanjali leaves no room for doubt when it comes to the *yamas*. They are non-negotiable. No aspiring yogi can progress without taking this "great vow" seriously.

You can't build a house with weak foundations. It will crumble. The *yamas* are the foundation of our yoga practice. Detachment and decent human behavior are necessary for the bare minimum peace of mind and focus needed to uncover the power of the mind.

32. The *niyamas* are cleanliness, satisfaction, study of sacred texts, grit and devotion to God.

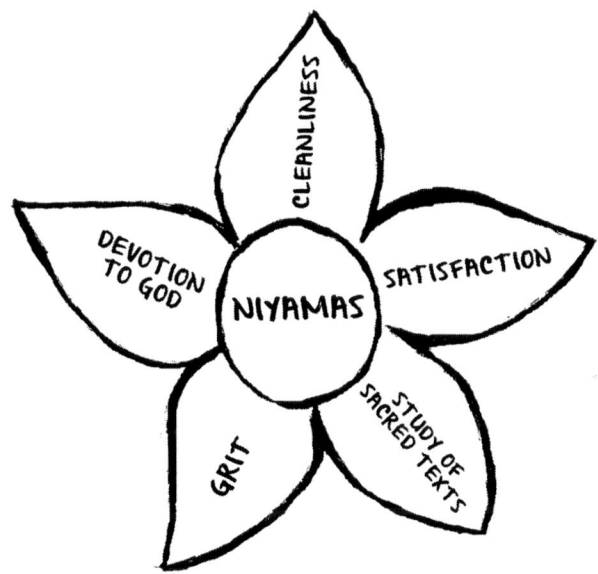

Yama refers to restraint. It means to *not* do something one might otherwise do. The *niyamas* refer to things that must be done, which otherwise one might not do.

Cleanliness is at the top of the list of the *niyamas*. This is because cleanliness activates *sattva*. If the mind is dominated by *sattva*, the yogi will experience peace, focus, and high levels of mental clarity—all necessary ingredients for spiritual advancement.

External cleanliness is achieved by taking practical steps to cultivate hygiene of your living and work space, clothes, and body. Internal cleanliness is achieved by first of all cultivating a friendly mood—a positive and helpful demeanor—to one and all. To pursue further internal cleanliness, the yogi attentively avoids feelings of envy, pride, vanity, anger, jealously, and hatred.

The proper practice of yoga naturally brings forth this internal cleanliness. As we focus on doing our best and expressing our essence and *dharma* in loving spiritual connection, no seed is planted to fructify into anxiety, jealousy, or vanity.

Satisfaction will also naturally arise from this practice. If one is focused not on external goals and material accomplishments but rather on one's own reaction to what life brings about, satisfaction is close at hand. It's easy to be satisfied by simply doing your best, according to your nature. But it's impossible to be satisfied when you're stuck in the Fantasy Paradigm of expecting external reality to be a certain way in order to be happy.

Note that the last three items of *niyama* are the same as those that define yoga in action, from Sutra 2.1, and you can refer to that sutra and the explanation of these key terms found there.

The only difference is that in Sutra 2.1 the word *tapa* was translated more loosely as "noble life." It means constantly prioritizing your higher self and aiming for spiritual progress over immediate sensory pleasure. The common but clumsy translation of this Sanskrit word is "austerity." For this sutra, I have opted to translate it as "grit." *Grit* is defined as courage, resolve, and strength of character. It's the power to stick to your path despite hardships. It means keeping your eye on the prize. Life isn't easy, and trying to become enlightened while dealing with it is harder still. The mind is impetuous and strong. Shaping your mind by the power of practice and sheer will requires enormous grit, as it's a tough, lifelong endeavor.

The *yamas* and *niyamas* are the cornerstones of yoga. They make for a life of high morals, careful behavior, detachment, satisfaction, cleanliness, and grit made transcendental by the two innermost components of yoga: study of the scriptures (*jnana*) and devotion to God (*bhakti*).

33. When harassed by a destructive mentality, the yogi must activate his or her spiritual intelligence.

34. Destructive mentality means that which is contrary to the *yamas* and *niyamas*. The yogi activates his or her spiritual intelligence by remembering that when an action is motivated by this destructive mentality, it will always result in continued suffering and ignorance. Any involvement with such actions, for any reason, is degrading. It doesn't matter if the action is carried out in person or by ordering or even allowing someone else to do it. And it doesn't matter if the degrading action is triggered by greed, anger, or illusion, nor whether it is mild, moderate, or extreme in intensity.

Patanjali leaves no wiggle room. This legal-contract-sounding sutra insists that the yoga practitioner take the *yamas* and *niyamas* seriously. No conditions exempt one from avoiding them or not having anything to do with them, even indirectly.

A serious yogi should take heed of this stern warning if he or she wishes to advance. It's my experience as both a practitioner and a teacher that Patanjali is not exaggerating. The *yamas* and *niyamas* are a summary of the entire process of yoga, and giving up any part of them will result in partial or complete failure.

35. Enmity is dissipated in the presence of a yogi established in nonviolence.

Patanjali will now list the boons for each of the *yamas* and *niyamas*. Our mood affects others. The more powerful our minds, the greater the effect. Advancing in yoga is good not only for us, but also for all those around us.

36. When truth is established, the yogi's actions and their results are firm.

Truth is solid. Lies easily fall apart. The more real and truthful we become, the more our actions are firmly grounded, and, consequentially, the more guaranteed and long-lasting the results are. Life is complicated enough without juggling lies.

37. When one ceases to steal, all riches become manifest.

When you become firm in the principle of honesty, you naturally radiate goodness and trustworthiness, which in turn attracts kind people to you and opens up doors for your business and work.

38. When chastity is established, the yogi gains power.

In the path of meditation-only yoga, celibacy is advocated as being a key ingredient for accumulating power. The concept is that celibacy prevents the loss of vitality, which can then be directed toward increased mental focus and the awakening of mystic powers (*vibhutis*).

For the rest of us, celibacy, like everything else on the yoga path, is good only if it's right for you. If being celibate is not natural to you, then the artificial restraint and suppression of sexual needs can corrode your well-being and lead to irritability, disease, and even violent behavior. Krishna alerts us in the *Bhagavad-gita* that one who restrains from activity without truly overcoming the desire deludes him- or herself and is a pretender.

In the path of enlightened life, those for whom celibacy is not suitable must direct their lives toward a sacred union, in which sex is a natural and wholesome act of love.

In this situation, the yogi will naturally acquire the power that comes from being true to him- or herself. By not living a lie or being corroded by frustration and unmet desires, you can unleash your true potential.

39. When non-possessiveness is established, the yogi understands how and why the soul becomes bound to take birth in a material body.

The yogi can understand that all of us are here incarnate due to material desires. It is attachment to things, and mundane experience in contact with things, that forces us to accept another material body at death. As long as we think happiness comes from the outside in, we'll need an "outside"—an external subsistence—and will be stuck in the illusion of life in the material world.

Non-possessiveness is a key realization needed for ultimate peace and bliss. The more you develop it, the freer—and thus the happier—you'll be.

40. When cleanliness of the body is established, the yogi develops aversion to his or her body and avoids intimate contact with others.

This may sound awful, but it's not. It just sounds strange because most people are still struggling with body-image issues and their own sexuality. They haven't even gotten to the point of being healthy and happy in their body, which would allow them to direct their focus inward, to their real identity.

Once you're in harmony with who you are and what body you have, you can continue to improve your life by raising your consciousness and focusing on your inner self. As your journey inward progresses, you'll find increasingly higher states of joy and peace, of fulfilment and satisfaction, in just being you and in your spiritual connection with everyone else, including God.

As a natural consequence, you'll understand that you're a fish out of water, an eternal blissful soul of pure transcendent energy stuck in a body made of matter. This is not home, and you are limited by your current circumstances, a prisoner of your past follies. It is in this regard that you develop a healthy dislike to being embodied.

At this stage of realization, a yogi gradually and naturally loses interest in having sexual contact with others, finding that to be less joyful and satisfying than just being by him- or herself. It's not that sex becomes bad or evil; it's that "just being" becomes so much better.

Artificially pretending to be at this stage will be harmful. Let it come to you naturally.

41. When cleanliness of the mind is established, the yogi develops cheerfulness, single-pointed focus, control of the senses, self-seeing, and qualification for yoga.

Your mind is your pathway to all success. It is your instrument to reach all your objectives. A mind free of confusion and agitation will naturally allow the self to shine through.

Cheerfulness is your default state. The soul is described in yoga as being made of *sat-cit-ananda*: existence-consciousness-bliss. Bliss is just who you are! We fail to experience it if we're not being ourselves but are deluded and buried under false identification and confusion.

Single-pointed focus is also natural to a clear mind. You have one mind, and it naturally has one focus. The clearer your mind is, the more you can practice single-pointed focus.

Control of the senses arises naturally when you can focus on being the best you can be, as opposed to focusing on external goals and future results. The more aligned you become with your true self and your *dharma*, the more easily you can navigate through life.

Self-seeing, or self-observation, require stillness of the mind. This is why silence and meditation are such powerful and necessary practices for the yogi. Just as you can see your reflection clearly on a body of still water but not if the water is choppy, so too you can see yourself clearly when your mind is still but not when it is agitated and disturbed.

A clear mind is the ultimate tool for the yogi and thus the ultimate qualification for achieving success in yoga.

42. From satisfaction, the highest happiness is achieved.

This might seem obvious. If you're satisfied, you're happy. What may not be so obvious is how to be satisfied.

Most people go about it all wrong. They mentally create external conditions that, if met, make them satisfied. For example, if I get that serving of ice cream, I'll be satisfied; if I get that new car, I'll be satisfied; or if that person behaves in such a way, I'll be satisfied.

The problem with setting up material requirements for satisfaction is two-fold: 1) the desires and conditions have little support—they change according to your whims, and 2) you have little to no control over future events, what to speak of how others will behave. As a result, if a desire is met, it often does little for your satisfaction level, because it wasn't really something you needed at your core. Plus, there is a good chance the desire won't be met at all, because the goal is not fully under your control.

The Fantasy Paradigm will always leave you feeling anxious and unfulfilled.

The alternative put forth by yoga is much more effective: hack your brain and put your "satisfaction" level on high. Just be satisfied. Not because of this or that. To the contrary, you can be satisfied precisely because you're no longer trying to squeeze satisfaction from external goals and events. You can take full satisfaction in just existing in the here and now. You don't need anything else.

Then you'll be happy.

43. From grit, impurities are removed and the body and senses achieve their perfection.

In the meditation-only path of yoga, it's necessary to live a life of renunciation and simplicity, a life dedicated exclusively to meditating, with no other distractions and practically no possessions. From these extreme measures, and the development of laser-like focus, such a yogi develops superpowers, which will be further explained in the next chapter.

On a more practical level, by having the grit to pursue yoga, one naturally develops discipline in eating, sleeping, work, and recreational activities. By basing your actions on what's best for you, not what's immediately most pleasurable, you can naturally maximize your health.

44. From the study of sacred texts, a connection with one's chosen Deity is established.

Knowledge (*jnana*) must precede devotion (*bhakti*). You can't love someone you don't know.

To enter the deeper aspect of pure self-realization in yoga, we must practice *jnana* and *bhakti*. Practicing *jnana* means studying the sacred

texts. The practice entails reading or listening to the texts and/or lectures on the texts. I recommend that you dedicate at least ten minutes daily to this practice. The more, the better.

As you absorb this wonderful sacred knowledge and wisdom, you gain the necessary ability to focus your mind and heart on God. As you learn about God, you can practice loving God, you can practice *bhakti*.

One might wonder about the meaning of "one's chosen Deity." In the West, God is God. No options are given, because very little information on God is provided in the Abrahamic traditions.

Not so in the Vedic tradition. There, a whole wealth of information is given about the nature of God, His abode, and His different expansions.

I present a more detailed explanation in *The 3T Path*; here I'll just share the basic concept.

The idea is that God has a personal form, known as *Bhagavan*. This *Bhagavan* form is God in His fullest aspect, demonstrating divine energy, form, and personality. Since God is infinite, He manifests innumerous *Bhagavan* forms simultaneously, each with a specific form, name, and abode and with specific associates and characteristics. In the sacred texts, you'll find descriptions of these various *Bhagavan* forms, as they come down as *avatars*, in different moments and places in the history of the universe.

The most well-known *Bhagavan* forms include Krishna, Narayana, and Rama, as well as Their female counterparts, Radha, Lakshmi, and Sita, respectively. The female counterparts are fully God as well, fully *Bhagavan*, but with female forms, names, and characteristics.

The "chosen Deity," then, is that *Bhagavan* form, or more precisely, the Divine Couple, which most attracts the heart of the devoted yogi.

Confused? Well, that's why study of the sacred texts is an essential part of yoga! In *The 3T Path*, you'll learn more about this and also find a comprehensive list of sacred texts to further your understanding.

45. From devotion to the Lord comes the perfection of *samadhi*.

There is no mincing of words here. Patanjali states clearly that the perfection of yoga comes from submission and dedication to the Lord. *Samadhi* is the perfection of yoga, which is the perfection of *samadhi*. In other words, the *perfection of the perfection* of yoga will come from devotion to God.

Love is the ultimate and highest expression of the soul. And loving an infinitely lovable, supremely wonderful, and unlimited Divine Person is the perfection of love. This is why devotion to God is the final perfection of existence.

If you're on uncertain terms with God, you might dislike this declaration. That's understandable, since God is often poorly represented. I too was an atheist, because the way God was presented to me was unappealing and because those claiming to love God often behaved poorly.

If that's the way you feel, you'll have to do two things.

First, discard all the crazy stuff you've heard about God. If you thought it was weird that God should hate gays or that He will torture you forever in Hell if you don't love Him, you're absolutely right. God is not into genocide, sexism, homophobia, torture, rape, or any of that evil stuff perpetrated in His name. Learn about God from the earliest and most complete source on the topic: the yoga tradition. Learn about God from this book, the *Bhagavad-gita*, and *Srimad-Bhagavatam*. You may be surprised to learn of a perfectly loving, kind, generous, compassionate, and charming God—exactly who you'd expect God to be.

Second, come to terms with the fact that devotion alone is not enough. Yoga offers a complete, holistic process for self-improvement and self-realization. Devotion is necessary to achieve the perfection of yoga, but it's not for nothing that the sacred texts on yoga explain a whole lot more. Devotion without the other *yamas* and *niyamas* can be dangerous. Devotion grants power, and power in the hands of those who are not dedicated to *ahimsa*, who lack self-control, is always dangerous. The long history and current practice of violence and horrors done by religious people is not God's fault, but rather the fault of those who have failed to understand and practice spiritual life in its entirety.

A simple analysis of what Krishna (God) identifies as the necessary qualifications for being an enlightened person leaves no room for doubt that a true devotee of God must be peaceful, compassionate, and well-wishing. This can be seen in the many lists of qualifications necessary for perfection in yoga, such as the *yamas* and *niyamas* in this text, the long list of wonderful qualities of a devotee of God in

Chapter Twelve of the *Bhagavad-gita*, and verses 1–3 of Chapter 16 also of the *Bhagavad-gita*.

This is why the yoga tradition has such a vital role to play in shaping spirituality on the global stage. As both individuals and parts of a collective whole, we need the full, sane, and practical instructions found in this tradition to overcome both soul-crushing materialism and hateful religious behavior.

46. The *asana* should be firm and easy.

Having finished the detailed description of each of the *yamas* and *niyamas*, Patanjali now moves on to the other limbs of *astanga-yoga*.

Very little is said about *asanas* in the *Yoga Sutras*. This is because the focus of yoga is the mind. I like the statement attributed to the famous eighth-century guru Sankara: "Mastery in *asanas* does not produce the goals of yoga, only getting rid of the obstacles to yoga."

Basically, the point of the *asana* is to have your body be in stand-by mode, allowing your mind to absorb your full attention for the practice of meditation. You have to forget your body, as it were. For that, you can neither be unsteady nor in pain.

To meditate, you should be steady and firm, yet comfortable.

47. This is attained by relaxing in the effort and absorbing the mind in the infinite.

Meditation is attained by the apparently contradictory combination of effort and relaxation. You have to push yourself and also let go.

Here Patanjali chose *ananta* as the word for the infinite. Another translation of this verse is that the yogi should absorb his or her mind in Ananta, become like Ananta, the cosmic snake form of the Lord. An expansion of God to serve God. It's God as the Servant of God, if you can wrap your mind around that.

One of the services provided by Ananta is to serve as God's seat. *Seat* in Sanskrit is "*asana.*" *Asana* is usually translated as "posture," but it literally means "seat." Ananta offers God a firm but comfortable seat. In Vedic Cosmology, Ananta also holds all the universes on his head; he is the seat of all the universes.

Patanjali is seen by many as an avatar of Ananta. As such, he is commonly portrayed as half-serpent, half-man. In this sense, Patanjali would be seen as Ananta serving the Lord as a preeminent yoga guru, helping establish this spiritual science.

48. Consequently, one becomes unaffected by duality.

The perfection of *asana* cuts the yogi off from all external bodily sensations. The mind becomes free to focus on its chosen object, indifferent to what is happening to the body.

In the Puranas, we find the drastic example of Hiranyakashipu, who so intently perfected his *asana* that he did not lose his focus even as his body was slowly consumed by ants and only his skeleton remained. And even then, he remained alive, with his *prana* circulating his bones. Don't try that at home.

49. In that state, *pranayama* can be achieved by regulating the incoming and outgoing breaths.

The fourth limb of *astanga-yoga* is *pranayama*, which literally means "control of breath."

Prana means more than just "air." It's synonymous with "life energy," or *qi* (chi) in the Chinese tradition.

Therefore, *pranayama* has the greater meaning of controlling our energy as a whole—the way we use our life.

50. *Pranayama* is defined in terms of external, internal, and restrained movements of breath. These can be deep or shallow. It means regulating where the breath will be held, for how long, and for how many cycles.

"External" means that you exhale and hold. "Internal" means you inhale and hold. And "restrained" is cessation of both, an in-between stage. These are further defined by how deep or shallow they are. *Pranayama* exercises will regulate where your breath is held, for how many counts, and for how many cycles.

51. A fourth type of breath goes beyond the limits of internal and external.

This is a further state of *prana* control that does not involve the physical inhalation and exhalation of air. In yoga literature, there is an abundance of description of yogis not breathing for extended periods of time. Some of these yogis would even practice underwater, for years at a time.

52. Then the covering of illumination is removed.

By the perfect control of our life's energy, we can become enlightened. In essence, yoga proposes a complete system for directing our body, mind, and soul, so we can properly channel our physical, mental, and spiritual energies.

53. Further, the mind becomes fit for concentration.

The sixth limb of *astanga-yoga* is now introduced, though it will be discussed in the next chapter. Patanjali mentions it here, before the fifth limb, to make the connection between mastery of *prana* and the three final, higher limbs of *astanga-yoga*. Everyone has experienced the direct connection between breathing and one's state of the mind. The best example of this is how we can relax and pacify our minds with deep steady breathing.

54. Withdrawal means turning your senses inward by disconnecting them from their sense objects. As a result, you'll experience the nature of the mind.

The fifth limb of *astanga-yoga* involves a withdrawal from the physical world, turning your focus inward. The senses unfasten from their sense objects: the eyes stop seeing forms, the nose stops smelling aromas, the skin stops experiencing touch.

As the senses are collected, like a turtle's limbs being retracting into its shell, the yogi is left to experience only the mind.

55. From this comes the greatest control of the senses.

The practical result of mastery in withdrawal is full control of the senses, a key component of yoga.

We must command our lives if we wish to find bliss and peace. A person who is not in control of his or her senses, is, by definition, controlled by them. In other words, the person is not in control of his or her life but instead is led this way and that by the whims of sense gratification. The only end results of such a hedonistic lifestyle are anxiety, depression, confusion, frustration, and pain.

Yoga is a call for you to take the helm. Be the captain of your ship and steer it to the blue waters of transcendental love, away from the rocky shores of suffering.

Vibhuti-pada

1. Concentration is fixing the mind in one place.

The last three limbs of *astanga-yoga* are about bringing the mind to a more precise and intense focus, a feat so extraordinary that it naturally bestows superpowers on the yogi. We will first learn the details of what this perfect focus of the mind entails and then the different superpowers yogis could attain and how it was done.

Before you get too excited and start planning your superhero outfit, be forewarned that the base requirement for achieving these powers is beyond the purview of just about anyone on the planet; it is the perfection of all previous limbs of *astanga-yoga* plus the ones about to be described. It entails having a perfectly peaceful mind in almost pure *sattva*, with total control of the body, vital energy, and mind.

While it's undeniable that you can still meet yogis with some small abilities, such as the ability to go without food or water for prolonged periods, or to start a fire with their vital energy, these are like child's play when compared with what will be described in this chapter and the accomplishments of great cosmic yogis of the past.

Our planet has changed. All the poison in our food, air, and water has damaged us. Perhaps being bombarded by radiation from radios, TV's, cellphones, microwaves, Wi-Fi, high-tension energy lines, and nuclear bomb tests has damaged our DNA and/or brains. Or perhaps the pace of modernity has destroyed the level of utter peace necessary for such a tranquil mind. Whatever the case, it doesn't seem like there are any yogis anymore with a wide range of truly impressive superpowers.

Skeptics may claim that it is all a lie, a bunch of tall tales. I don't think so. There are just too many accounts from too many sources throughout the ages.

But regardless, the point is that lack of power is not our problem; we already have enough of that. Our problem is not knowing how to live well and yield the power we already have. Technology has allowed us to fly, go to space and deep underwater, survive in heat and cold extremes, and heal our bodies. We hear and see from across great distances and have instant access to vast storehouses of knowledge. Unfortunately, in our use of all this power, we're mostly just killing each other, making ourselves miserable, and destroying the planet.

That is why we need to focus on the path of enlightened life, not the path of meditation-only yoga. It will certainly make your life better and, as more people take to it, bring new hope for humanity.

2. Meditation is fixing the mind on a single point.

Concentration is a general area of focus, while meditation is a single point, image, or thought without distraction or interruption.

Think of a beam of light with a variable focus. Concentration is like a common flashlight. Meditation, the seventh limb of *astanga-yoga*, is a laser point.

3. *Samadhi* is when meditation is focused on the object alone and the yogi forgets him- or herself.

This sutra describes the eighth and final limb of *astanga-yoga*: *samadhi*. *Samadhi* is super-meditation. It's the perfection of meditation. It's total absorption on the object of meditation to the point where the meditator is no longer aware of him- or herself. The focus on the object is so great that nothing registers in the yogi's mind.

On the path of enlightened life, *samadhi* will manifest itself in a different way. Obviously, one cannot forget him- or herself, what to speak of other people, cars, and buildings, as you go about your life. *Samadhi* as described in this sutra can be done only while sitting in a remote spot in the wilderness.

The perfection of yoga on the path of enlightened life means to never have your mind deviate from God, your true nature as a soul, your *dharma*, or the here and now. Even as you go about, aware of your body, home, children, work, and car, you maintain your absorption in the ultimate transcendental reality of life.

That's still remarkably difficult, maybe even seemingly impossible, but it's doable. And it's not all or nothing. The more you do it, the better your life will be.

4. When these three are combined, it's called *samyama*.

A new term is presented here: *samyama*, which can be translated as "perfect discipline." *Samyama* is achieved by practicing the last three stages of *astanga-yoga*. It is this combination that will be used to harness different superpowers, according to the different objects of meditation employed by the yogi.

5. From *samyama* comes pure wisdom.

Natural wisdom arises from pacifying the mind, even on a very basic level. Silence holds many answers. The more you pacify and silence your mind and the greater your ability to focus your mind on the divine, the more your doubts will evaporate and clarity will set in.

6. This is applied in different stages.

Realizations come in stages. It's like gradually opening your eyes. Or climbing a mountain and gradually seeing further and further away. It's an amazing journey and a wondrous experience to live like this, gaining increasing vision with the passage of time. At every step, new realizations materialize. You'll experience this from day one, and it won't stop as long as you keep progressing.

7. In contrast to the other five, these three are internal limbs of yoga.

Patanjali calls concentration, meditation, and *samadhi* the internal limbs of yoga, as they pertain exclusively to the art of focusing the mind on an object, with progressively greater intensity. The first five elements describe the relationship between the self and the world, including God.

8. Yet, even these three are external to seedless *samadhi*.

Ultimately, we are spiritual souls, meant to live a life of endless variety and bliss with God in His abode. Yoga is the cure for the disease of being incarnate and confused. Once the disease is gone, there is no more need for treatment.

9. Control of the mind is achieved gradually, as subliminal impressions of such an enlightened stage substitute those of worldly activity.

Patanjali stated that the goal of yoga is control of the mind. Once the mind is under our control, we can command our life to our full advantage, ultimately becoming liberated in pure divine love.

In this section, Patanjali describes the technical details of how this process comes about.

As will be further explained, yoga claims that our minds express our nature and that our nature is composed of the countless subliminal impressions we have thus far experienced. You act or think according to what you have experienced and what is registered in your subconscious mind.

One way to look at the process of yoga is to gradually replace mundane subliminal impressions with enlightened moments. Think of it as rewriting your mind's hard-drive. Old data pertaining to bodily egocentric experiences is gradually written over, with new data recording your moments of focus on the here and now, following your *dharma*, and experiencing communion with God.

Every moment counts. Every second you can be in the right yogic frame of mind is one more byte rewritten.

As you accumulate these subliminal impressions, you naturally become more inclined to perform them again, reinforcing them still further, in an upward spiral of spiritual consciousness.

10. The mind's peaceful flow will come from these enlightened subliminal impressions.

As you advance in yoga, the mind will naturally and peacefully stay connected, on "the mind's peaceful flow." Being in a flow as you're kayaking down a waterfall or performing on stage is amazing, but being in this peaceful flow of yoga is even better.

11. Transformation toward *samadhi* involves reducing moments of lack of focus and increasing the moments of single-pointed focus.

This sutra describes another type of transformation, this one regards the focus of the mind. Patanjali uses the Sanskrit term meaning "all objects" in contrast to "one object." He is comparing your distracted mind thinking of a million things to your mind fully focused on one thing at a time.

12. This single-pointed focus means that the new image entering the mind is the same as the previous one.

The mind is in constant flow; life never stops. So, to have a stable single-pointed focus in the meditation-only branch of yoga means that at every instant the same image, or thought, enters the mind. It's not that the mind stops. In this sense, the mind is like a movie, not a picture gallery. Single-pointed focus means a movie with the same frame repeated for the duration of the meditation.

In the path of enlightened life, single-pointed focus has a more general connotation of not letting your guard down. It means being active in the here and now, in your dharma, and in loving connection with God. No mean feat. It takes a lot of focus and a great deal of practice to do that consistently.

13. This is how transformations in characteristics, properties, and conditions in material elements and sense organs are explained.

Yoga sees the material world as being made up not only of atoms, but of *gunas*, the modes of material nature. Everything in the universe is a transformation of the same material energy. Stars and lollipops are ultimately made of the same substance. It's all in motion, never static, and always subject to change. We know this now for a scientific fact, but yogis knew since time immemorial.

The perfect meditation-only yogi would be able to fuse his or her mind with this substratum of reality and thus manipulate it at will. What yogis would do with their minds, modern man does with technology and intelligence: manipulate energy and matter.

14. Things seem to change as a result of their properties changing in the past, present, and future.

Things seem to change, but they are the same. Atoms move about, molecules bond, and properties change, but the point is that there is a substratum of reality that is unchanging. It's all the same material energy.

15. The change of these properties causes transformation.

Patanjali has now explained the basic theory behind yogic superpowers. The concept is familiar to us, as it's the same concept behind modern science. Reality shares common building blocks; thus, things can be manipulated and transformed.

Patanjali's Guide to Superpowers

The rest of this chapter is dedicated to listing different superpowers. The basic idea is that full single-pointed focus on different objects of meditation—be they parts of the body, metaphysical concepts, or natural occurrences—causes the yogi to acquire a specific superpower.

If, like everyone else on the planet, you haven't quite mastered single-pointed focus, this section won't be very helpful, but it's fascinating nonetheless.

16. *Samyama* on the three transformations grants the power to know past, present, and future.

The three transformations were described above. They are:

1) Transformation of substituting mundane subliminal impressions with enlightened ones,

2) Transformation toward *samadhi* and single-pointed focus, and

3) Transformation of material things, while the substratum remains the same.

17. Confusion arises from erroneously considering word, meaning, and idea to be the same. *Samyama* **on the distinction between them grants the power to understand the speech of all animals.**

We tend to classify an idea, name, and object as one. Pick an object in front of you. Now try to separate the object into the idea of the thing, its name, and the unlabeled thing itself.

18. Directly perceiving subliminal impressions grants knowledge of previous births.

One way to think of this is straightforward: the more you perceive your nature, inclinations, and conditionings, the more you can understand where you're coming from. The yogic version just takes it further by granting clear knowledge of other births.

19. Perceiving other people's ideas grants knowledge of their minds.

All of us have this power to some extent. We can all read some people some of the time. The yogic version implies knowing people deeply and much more accurately and all of the time.

20. This knowledge does not include knowledge of the object of their thoughts, since that object is not the yogi's object.

Even a powerful yogi cannot read your mind, know exactly what you're thinking. Instead, the yogi has a general idea of mood, emotions, and inclinations.

21. *Samyama* on the outer form of the body grants the power of invisibility. This is done by blocking the light reflecting off the body from reaching the eyes of the observer.

Just as technology has produced surfaces that do not reflect radar, making them invisible to radar, so too the yogi could change the quality of his or her outer body to not reflect light, making him or her invisible.

Of course, now that we're all so self-absorbed and engrossed in our smartphones, everyone is pretty much invisible.

22. Some karmic reactions are happening now, and some will happen in the future. *Samyama* on karma and on omens grants knowledge of death.

For those of us who cannot know exactly when or how we'll die, it's best to always be prepared. A yogi should regularly remind him- or herself that life can end at any moment. We cannot take tomorrow for granted. Our life and the lives of everyone we know can end at any moment. This knowledge helps us keep our focus on our true spiritual nature and make the most of every day, as well as make the most of every opportunity to love and serve those around us.

23. *Samyama* on friendliness, etc. grants their powers.

In Sutra 1.33, Patanjali listed four characteristics a yogi should cultivate: 1) friendliness, 2) compassion, 3) joy in piety and 4) indifference to impiety. Now, he says that *samyama* on each of these grants the yogi with these respective characteristics and their powers.

24. *Samyama* on any power grants the yogi that power. For example, *samyama* on the strength of an elephant grants the yogi with the strength of an elephant.

Patanjali states that for the perfected yogi, the law of attraction works instantly. This *sutra* states that whatever power the yogi wishes to possess, he or she will possess. Strength, speed, intelligence, heat, cold… powers are transferable immediately at the request of the yogi.

25. Directing light to the power of perception grants knowledge of things that are subtle, concealed, or distant.

This power arises without the need for *samyama*. Because of the yogi's powerful, clear mind, merely directing his or her attention to something, even if it is subtle, concealed, or distant, allows him or her to perceive it. The modern term for this power is *remote viewing*. There is enough of this going on even today to account for extensive research. There are even websites dedicated to teaching this ability.

26. *Samyama* on the sun grants knowledge of different worlds.

There is a fascinating presentation of the universe in the Indic tradition, with detailed descriptions of different worlds and alien civilizations.

27. *Samyama* on the moon grants knowledge of star constellations.

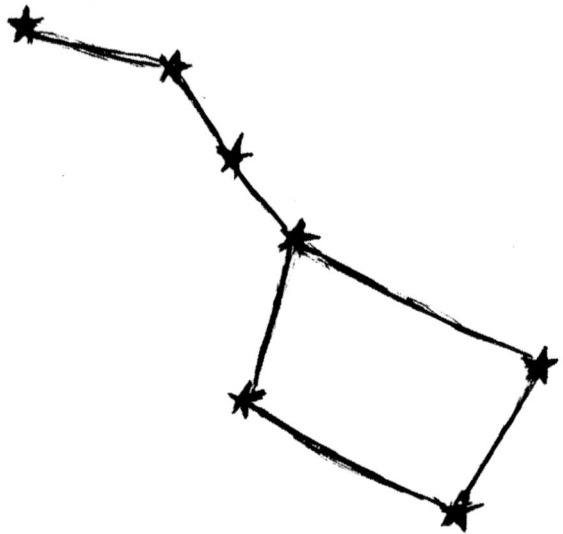

28. *Samyama* on the pole star grants knowledge of the movement of the stars.

29. *Samyama* on the navel chakra grants knowledge of the workings of the body.

30. *Samyama* on the throat cavity grants freedom from hunger and thirst.

The most famous modern case of this superpower is that of Prahlad Jani, who made headlines earlier this century when he claimed to have had nothing to eat or drink for seventy years. Even after putting him through controlled observation for fifteen days in a hospital, during which time he consumed no water or food of any sort, doctors could still not explain how that was possible.

31. *Samyama* on the "tortoise channel" grants steadiness.

The *kurma-nadi* is a channel of *prana*, shaped like a tortoise, below the pit of the throat. *Prana* is said to move around the body in channels, much like blood moves around the body in veins.

This power allows the yogi to remain perfectly still, both externally and mentally.

32. *Samyama* on the light in the head grants vision of perfected beings.

In the sophisticated and detailed cosmology of the Indic tradition, there is mention of many races. Here the *siddhas* or "perfected beings" are mentioned. They are a race of highly advanced benevolent beings, naturally gifted with all kinds of mystical powers, including the power to travel freely throughout the universe.

33. By intuition comes everything.

Intuition here means the pre-dawn of near omniscience brought about by spiritual liberation. As the yogi nears perfect *sattva*, all his or her doubts are dispelled. In this state, all previously mentioned powers also become manifest.

34. *Samyama* on the heart grants knowledge of the mind.

In both Eastern and Western cultures, the heart has long been seen as the seat of the real you, the soul. As you focus on your nature, on this real you, you gain knowledge of both your mind and consciousness itself.

Krishna makes this connection in *Srimad-Bhagavatam*, in the *Uddhava-gita* section, where He connects the practice of *dharma* with the cultivation of *jnana*. He claims that by cultivating your essence and duty, you naturally attain realization of your true spiritual identity.

In *The 3T Path*, I also recommend strong focus on your *dharma* as a central means for your spiritual development and to increase emotional and physical well-being.

35. In the mundane view, there is no difference between the personal spiritual identity and *sattva*, although these are entirely different. *Sattva* exists for the soul, yet the soul stands on its own, with no need of material nature. *Samyama* on the soul grants knowledge of the personal spiritual identity.

In essence, this sutra describes the whole goal of yoga. Yoga serves to free our spiritual selves from our false identification with material nature. The purpose of yoga is to allow you to become your true, spiritual, personal self again. All our pain is due to our false identification with that which is not us. Material energy, even in its luminous *sattva* state, is nothing like spiritual energy. To put it simply, people and things are different.

36. This knowledge enables an intuitive higher form of hearing, feeling, seeing, tasting, and smelling.

37. These powers are obstacles to pure spiritual perfection. They take the mind out instead of in.

This is the first sutra with stern warnings on how foolish it is to want any power to manipulate the external world. To desire such superpowers is directly opposed to what yoga is all about: learning to change your interpretation of life, not life itself. In yoga, we learn that our real happiness depends not on what life brings us, but on what we make of it. Power corrupts, and using superpowers is sure to corrupt the mind of even the kind of highly accomplished yogi capable of developing them.

In contrast, the path of enlightened life in yoga, where such superpowers do not arise, is more practical, sensible, attainable, and favorable.

38. By loosening the bonds to the body and by knowledge of the pathways of the mind, the yogi can partially possess the bodies of others.

By this power, the yogi can enter the body of another person, experiencing what they experience and manipulating what they say and do. There are many accounts of this found in Indic literature. The yogi's body remains in suspension, awaiting the return of his or her mind to the body.

39. Mastery over the rising flow of *prana* grants the power of levitation, and with this, the yogi does not sink into water, mud, thorns, etc.

Walking on water, moving objects, being indifferent to harsh physical abuse, and even raising the dead are all yogic powers. This is one reason why people suspect that Jesus spent time in India training in meditation-only yoga during the twenty unaccounted-for years of his life. This is also why people accustomed to the Indic tradition are less impressed by the "miracles" performed by Jesus than by his powerful love of God. Miracles are a dime a dozen in the yoga tradition, but intense and pure love of God has always been cherished as the supreme goal of existence.

40. Mastery over the digestive *prana* grants a fiery radiance.

These descriptions of yogic superpowers may explain the superhuman behavior and aura surrounding saints and divine figures of other religions. *Yoga Sutras* commentators of old explain that some of these powers arise without bidding.

41. *Samyama* on the connection of the ear and space grants divine hearing.

42. *Samyama* on the connection of the body and space and intense concentration on the lightness of cotton grants the ability to fly.

The concept is that as the yogi gains power, he or she can develop the ability to walk on water, then on subsequently lighter materials, such as spider-webs, then air, then beams of sunlight. This ability is not limited to flying around this planet. There are many stories of yogis doing interplanetary travel.

43. That state of mind that is fully outside and not imagined is called the great out-of-body experience. With this, the covering of light is destroyed.

It's hard to say if this state bears resemblance to claims of out-of-body experiences detailed in innumerable websites and books. The concept, however, is clear. The yogi has the full experience of existing beyond his or her body, essentially living out the sought-after realization that he or she is not the body, but an eternal, non-material personal entity.

44. *Samyama* on the external, intrinsic, subtle, constitutional, and purposive nature of matter grants power over them.

This sutra sums up how the yogic superpowers work, but it could just as well be an explanation of how science and technology create the miracles we're accustomed to today. The concept is the same. By closely studying and understanding the many layers of material nature, one can manipulate its properties.

The difference is that the yogi would depend exclusively on the power of his or her thoughts, which is arguably a more refined and precise tool than any we can find in factories or laboratories. As a result, the yogi could bring about changes in nature that we cannot yet do with science and technology. Of course, the downside is that it's fantastically difficult to learn this trade and that once the yogi has gone, all the gains have gone as well, whereas with technology, all the gains are shared and built upon, giving rise to exponential growth of collective technological prowess.

45. With this, superpowers arise, such as the classic eight starting with atomic size, total bodily perfection, and freedom from the constraints of the laws of nature.

There are eight classic superpowers mentioned in Indic literature:

1. Becoming atomic in size;
2. Making the body as light as air;
3. Becoming as gigantic and heavy as desired;
4. Being able to grab or attain anything desired from anywhere in the universe;
5. Being able to materialize any desire;
6. Having power over all the elements and other living beings;
7. Having the power to manipulate matter, making it appear, disappear or rearranging it as desired;
8. Holding Lordship over material nature, making things do whatever is desired.

46. Bodily perfection means having beauty, charm, and the strength of a thunderbolt.

47. *Samyama* on the ability to learn, on one's true form, on the ego, and on the constitution and purpose of material nature grants power over the senses.

The progressively finer focus on the nature of existence of the yogi's own body grants that yogi power over the senses.

48. This entails being able to move at the speed of the mind, being able to acquire knowledge and act independently of the body, and having mastery over the essence of nature.

As the chapter nears its end, the superpowers reach their zenith in what is basically a claim to omnipotence and omniscience.

49. Only for those who can perfectly discern the difference between *sattva* and spirit can omnipotence and omniscience be achieved.

The real goal of yoga is again mentioned here: perfect discernment between matter and spirit. In other words, illumination meant to completely cease identification with matter and allow one to exist as a pure spiritual soul.

50. By being indifferent even to these superpowers, all the seeds of bondage are destroyed and *kaivalya*, perfect spiritual freedom, is attained.

Ultimately, it's a test. As seen in the stories of Jesus and Buddha, a true spiritualist most overcome all temptations. Yoga offers a supreme menu of unimaginable temptations, right up to the point of one practically becoming God. Those who fall for it fall from grace. In the end, it's a simple question of asking, "What do you want?" Is it mundane power? Or eternal spiritual liberation and bliss?

Imagine that you've been playing video games for too long. It's become a problem, and you decide that it's all a big waste of time. You decide that you want to live life for real again. You want to do sports, get a job, meet people, or travel. But then you're offered power-ups in your game—new weapons, a new more exciting version. Is that going to weaken your will? Are you going to give up getting your life together again in exchange for the illusory joy of more power and new levels in your video game?

We're all living a powerful virtual-reality game called *samsara*. Our bodies and minds serve as the interface; the universe is the playing field. Total immersion. Very convincing. But life outside the matrix is better, and now we want to quit. We want to go home and get our lives back.

So, get your head straight. Be focused and sure of what you want. Because if you're still into playing this game, you won't have sufficient drive, grit, or focus to win your freedom through yoga. In the words of the wise Queen Kunti, Krishna's aunt and the mother of the Pandavas, you must be "materially exhausted" to attain spiritual perfection, *kaivalya*.

51. Celestial beings will tempt the yogi to their realms. The yogi should deny them and not allow even such an invitation to instill pride in them. Otherwise, harmful attachments will again surge.

Heavenly planets abound, and the denizens of these places will come and tempt the yogi with citizenship in their realms. There, the yogi would receive a beautiful celestial body; unlimited opportunities for gorgeous and willing sex companions; celestial food, palaces, gardens; and perfect health care. But the yogi must turn down the invitation, knowing it to be a temporary distraction in the game of *samsara*. Not only that; the yogi cannot even feel pride or smugness in having been invited, for that too would feed his or her dark side.

52. *Samyama* on the moment and the movement of time grants knowledge born of discrimination.

Viveka, commonly translated as "discrimination," is a key term in the *Yoga Sutras*, referring to the ultimate spiritual ability to discriminate matter from spirit. It's the knowledge that allows the soul to extricate itself from its entanglement in matter.

Matter is constantly in flux. At every moment, atoms are moving about from one position to another. Spirit is unmovable, unchangeable, and eternal. Thus, by full meditation on the fact that time affects only matter, one can realize one's spiritual nature.

53. With this, the yogi can tell apart two things that seem otherwise identical in terms of origin, characteristic, and position.

With mastery over time, the yogi can perceive the "history" of an object on the atomic level. Thus, he or she can distinguish between two apparently identical things. The modern equivalent of this is using a powerful microscope or other scientific instrument.

54. Knowledge born of discrimination grants spiritual liberation and is all-inclusive and timeless.

Spiritual wisdom surpasses everything in reality and goes beyond the past, present, and future.

Now we close the cycle. We became entangled in material reality, but through yoga we disentangle ourselves by carefully understanding the difference between us and matter.

In terms of the presentation in this book, there is also a cycle being closed here.

Patanjali stated back in 2.28 that the goal of yoga is to attain *viveka*, which grants liberation. He mentions this, strategically, just before beginning his explanation of *astanga-yoga*, the meditation-only path of yoga, after having explained the general, enlightened life path.

Now, having explained the process and results of this intense, difficult process, he reminds the reader what it is all about: *viveka*.

Note, however, that *viveka* requires neither any superpower nor the practice of *astanga-yoga*.

This same goal of *viveka* and liberation can be achieved naturally by the practice of the path of enlightened life.

55. When *sattva* is in perfect balance with the soul, *kaivalya* occurs.

When the yogi cleanses his or her mind entirely of the other *gunas*, having only *sattva* shining forth, the mind finally becomes a flawless and clear mirror to perfectly reflect the soul. At this point, the yogi has achieved perfect self-realization and is thus liberated for all eternity, never to come back to material existence. In the *Yoga Sutras*, this state of liberation is called *kaivalya*.

Kaivalya-pada

1. These superpowers may also come by birth, herbs, mantras, austerities, and *samadhi*.

By good karma, one can be born with all kinds of facilities, including mystic superpowers.

We have experience of how drugs can augment human capabilities. In the sacred texts, we see that mantras too could be used as magic spells. Queen Kunti received such a mantra from the powerful but short-tempered yogi Durvasa Muni, who was endowed with the full range of yogic superpowers. With her mantra, Queen Kunti could summon any *deva* to beget children, giving rise to the birth of the five Pandavas, the central characters of the *Mahabharata*, in which we find the *Bhagavad-gita*.

Here the word *austerities* implies a sort of mortification of the body, such as prolonged periods of self-imposed discomfort, like standing on one leg, enduring near self-starvation, or exposing oneself to great heat or cold, as we saw in the example of Hiranyakashipu.

And powers may come from *samadhi*, without yearning for it, or without a special *samyama*. There are many accounts of spiritualists from different traditions with special powers.

The important point here is that superpowers are not in themselves a sign of spiritual development. They may arise from it, but they are neither the goal of spiritual life nor a sign of spiritual progress. Many ill-informed spiritual seekers get fooled by such things.

2. The change in body from one birth to another is shaped by material energy.

Having spoken of births in the previous sutra, Patanjali explains that we transmigrate from one body to another, with material energy filling out our new body.

Our material desires and karmic reactions accumulate in our consciousness. As the physical body dies before these are exhausted, another one must be created to continue the process. Thus, the soul is trapped in an endless cycle of birth and death until, with yoga, it can forcefully and consciously put an end to the process.

3. Material energy is not caused by itself but happens by forces beyond the covering of the universe, such as a field being worked by a farmer.

A crop is not the result of merely the crop itself, or the field. Its ultimate cause is the farmer, whose energy and intent make it happen. The material energy that encompasses our experience when we are embodied beings is not caused by material energy. The Divine Farmer, God, causes it to happen from beyond the universe.

4. Individual thoughts are the result of one measure of ego.

Every thought you have is the result of who you are. It comes up from your nature, be it conscious or unconscious. You don't have other people's thoughts; you have thoughts that pertain only to who *you* are. Each thought is like a drop of the ocean of your current nature.

5. A single thought produces many thoughts and/or actions.

Our thoughts bring about other thoughts and actions in an apparently endless sequence.

These other thoughts and actions then shape our nature. Neuroscience confirms that everything you do and think changes your brain. As you change, a measure of your ego will also change, leading to new and different thoughts and actions.

Your constantly changing set of thoughts and actions will lead to the creation of a new physical body suited to your nature at the time of death.

6. A thought born of meditation, however, is karma-free.

Spiritual thoughts and actions do not entangle the yogi. They free the yogi from his or her karma and gradually eliminate his or her material ego.

Every moment you elevate your thoughts to your divine nature, keeping your mind in the here and now and living out your *dharma*, creates a permanent subliminal register of perfection. This changes your nature from mundane to spiritual, one measure at a time. As your nature is thus changed, you become more able to have elevated thoughts, and they, in turn, become a greater part of your nature. Life in yoga may have a rough start, but, in a virtuous circle of purification, it becomes increasingly easier with time. Your efforts are thus richly compensated.

Krishna says in the *Bhagavad-gita* that actions in *sattva* are like poison in the beginning but like nectar in the end.

7. A yogi's action is neither white nor black. Those of others are white, black, and all shades in between.

A yogi no longer accumulates karma. Karma can be good or bad, here referred to as white or black. Good karma grants good material situations and facilities. Bad karma causes adverse situations and suffering. It's not just black or white, though; it's all shades in between. The complexities of karma are immense, so each non-yogic action comes with an indiscernible mix of reactions.

The initial focus of yoga is to stop generating karma. In the early chapters of the *Bhagavad-gita*, Krishna makes this a leading topic to introduce and explain yoga. In the *Yoga Sutras*, it's not a major theme, but it is important enough to be mentioned in this section on karma.

The concept can be simply explained:

1. If you identify with an action and *desire its result*, you voluntarily sign up for karma. You ask for it, but there's a lot of fine print. You get a lot more than you could imagine, and some results can take a lot longer to fructify than you may have thought possible—even lifetimes.
2. The quality of your karmic reaction is based on the *dharmic* quality of the action. The truer it is to your *dharma*, the "whiter" the reaction. When you get it right, you get positive feedback. When you get it wrong, you unknowingly put in a request for training. The universe will comply, setting you up to experience the mirror experience of the situation you failed in—reversing roles, as it were. You'll

get a chance to see why it was wrong—a taste of your own medicine. But white, black, or any shade in between, you're still stuck in *samsara*. You're trapped in the cycle of birth and death. And because karma is so complex and the nature of being incarnated is so difficult, you're bound to always suffer. The yogi figures that out and learns to quit the whole karmic game.

3. The way to quit the game is two-fold: first, you must stop accumulating karma, and second, you must burn up the karma you've already accumulated.

4. You stop accumulating karma by *not desiring the result*. You keep your mind in the here and now and bring your focus to your *dharma*: "What is the best action now?" Be totally present in the action, doing your very best, according to your nature. Then offer that to God. Identify not with your body, your material situation, or the action. Identify yourself instead with your divine nature and your source, God. You'll then naturally act for the pleasure of doing your best, or, in devotional terms, for the pleasure of God. This is called *karma-yoga*, and it's the core guiding principle in the path of enlightened life.

5. You burn up your karma with knowledge and introspection. You cultivate transcendental wisdom and absorb the transcendent nature of existence. You understand why *sattva* is important, why *dharma* is essential, and who and what you really are. You see where you are, where you have come from, and where you are going. As you understand all these things, you render unnecessary any future training

programs you had previously invoked. No more need for training. You got it. You understand. You "test out" of any future material situation.

Then there is love. As this is all happening, you're increasingly becoming pure and your loving nature comes forth. *Bhakti* shines through, and you fall in love with God and other pure souls. Free of karma, you go home to the transcendental abode to forever act in love and endless joy.

8. Only a set of those reactions is activated in the next life.

Part of what makes karma so complex is the scale of time. Actions in one lifetime can generate reactions many lifetimes later. This is why we see bad things happening to apparently good people and good things happening to apparently bad people. In truth, everyone is getting exactly what they need and deserve, but to understand this, you have to step back and look beyond what is perceivable. No one who took birth is so innocent, nor so evil. We all carry within us the seeds of good and evil. Only God knows what we've done in the past. This is our chance to get it right. Now we can clean the slate and learn once and for all how to live like a loving soul.

9. Subliminal impressions and memories are not interrupted by birth, time, or place.

Karma and subliminal impressions are carried forth from one birth to another, over time and space. These outwardly changes do not erase your previous experiences.

Your inner nature won't change if you change cities, marry, or even die. You have to change your nature by your active, direct intervention. Moving to a different city or country won't make you different. Waiting to become a better person won't work. Committing suicide because you hate the person you are won't cure your problems. You're still going to be you.

Human life is the chance you get to become better. Right now, you have the means to make a difference and work off your bad habits, selfishness, anger, greed, anxiety, and lack of compassion.

Yoga gives you the chance to dig deep and clear out all the trash in your heart. But you have to make it happen. Procrastination will only add to your troubles, and you may miss out on this rare and wonderful opportunity.

10. Subliminal impressions are eternal because the desires are eternal.

Here the word *eternal* is used in the sense of "without an end in sight." The desires that keep you reincarnating can be ended, and that is yoga's objective. But they will only come to an end if you take an active stance to make them end. If not, they'll go on "without an end in sight."

The gist of it is that material nature and embodied life are set up in a looping system. *Samsara* is often portrayed as a wheel. A circle has no beginning and no end. Our life in illusion, in false identification, has been going on and on—one desire to another, one body to another, one era to another, in endless cycles. Yoga equips you with all the tools you need to make this stop, which you and only you can do. You have to want it, and you have to make it happen with a ton of grit. It's a wonderful journey, though, and you'll be richly compensated at every step of the way.

11. Subliminal impressions are maintained by cause and effect. When these are eliminated, the subliminal impressions are also eliminated.

Actions generate reactions. And as you react to the reactions, you act again, and the cycle continues. This is the cause-and-effect motor that keeps us trapped in *samsara*.

But we can break the cycle. This is done by not acting with material desire, but instead acting with the sole desire to live your *dharma* in divine connection. Bringing your mind to the divine in the here and now breaks the cycle. Once you've achieved this elevated mindset, you've permanently broken the cycle. This is how liberation is achieved.

12. Past and future exist in the now, in the change of characteristics through time.

As a careful observer of the present, the yogi can perceive past and future. Just as scientists can discern the past and predict future results by studying the characteristics of different objects and systems, so too the yogi can get an increasingly clear feel of where things are coming from and where they are going.

13. The *gunas*, either manifest or latent, are the essence of the past, present, and future.

As explained earlier, in yoga metaphysics the *gunas* are the substratum of all material reality. The idea here is that the material energy is the same and changes only its external qualities, such as shape, but it does not change its essence. To put it another way, the passage of time does not modify the constituents of reality, only their configuration.

14. Because of this essence, though things change, they are real.

You'll see the word *illusion* used frequently in this and other yoga texts. But yoga does not claim that the entirety of matter is illusion. It is all real. The universe does exist outside your mind.

The illusion we must avoid is in identifying our spiritual nature with material nature. *Viveka*, remember? Our spiritual journey is us untangling ourselves from matter. Two divine energies: matter and consciousness. But we are conscious entities, souls. Matter has no consciousness. We do. Simple as that. Figure out the difference, stop the illusionary identification, and you're home free.

Krishna says in the *Bhagavad-gita* that the *gunas* are His "divine energy." Then He explains that because He's the boss of the *gunas*, we would do well to accept His help in getting untangled from them. Makes sense. And it works.

15. Because different minds perceive the same object differently, there is a difference between the object and the mind.

Individual minds exist, proving that we're individual, unique observers. Further, since different observers perceive things differently, what we perceive is also different from us, and from every other observer.

I exist, you exist, and so does everything you observe. There is a connection between all of us and everything, but there is also a distinction.

16. Does not an object still exist, even if unobserved?

Heard of Schrödinger's cat? Quantum physics? I'm not going to get into it here, but this question isn't as strange as you might imagine.

Patanjali is trying to point out that reality is not subjective. The view of yoga is that reality exists on its own ground and need not be observed to be real.

17. A thing is known or not known by the mind, depending on how the mind has been tinged by it.

Basic stuff here, in line with what we generally think of as true: something that exists will only be known if the mind is directed to it, if you focus on it. The more you focus on it, the more you'll know it. If you don't direct your mind to it at all, you won't know it at all.

Yoga won't try to blow your mind away with the-sound-of-one--hand-clapping stuff. Yoga keeps it real.

18. The fluctuations of the mind are known to its master, the soul, for it never changes.

External reality is real and independent of our minds. Minds are always changing, so they see reality differently. But each mind has a master, the individual personal soul, to witness it. And that soul, the real you, never changes, being eternal and transcendental in nature.

People often ask me, "If the soul is eternal and unchanging, how come I feel so much change, especially now that I'm on this path of yoga?" "You're not changing," I reply. "It's your mind that's changing. You were always the same. Your mind is never the same." The feeling of advancing spiritually comes from experiencing your mind letting you increasingly experience your true self, by getting out of the way.

19. The mind does not illuminate itself, as it's an object of perception.

The mind cannot illuminate itself. The mind is the instrument of the soul. Though hard to grasp, the yoga concept is that the mind is part of the material world, an element of nature, like earth and water. Because of this, it can be perceived, and, like everything else in material nature, it is constantly changing.

The simplest and best way to understand the mind is to see it as a mirror that reflects whatever is directed at it, be it mundane objects or the real you.

The process of self-realization is thus described by the medieval avatar Krishna Chaitanya Mahaprabhu as "cleaning the dust of the mirror."

20. Both thought and object cannot be perceived at the same time.

You can focus your attention on your thoughts or you can focus your attention on an external object, but not both at the same time.

Yoga has been saying this for thousands of years, and now science confirms it: there is no such thing as multi-tasking. Your brain can focus on only one thing at a time, be it some thought or emotion you want to process, or something external. The feeling of multi-tasking is an illusion of fast switching. Your brain will switch from, say, driving to speaking to someone, and then back. That's why driving and talking on your phone, even with a full hands-free system, is very dangerous: studies show you might be a full second slower to respond.

The result of what we call multi-tasking is that instead of doing more, you'll be less efficient and perform less well.

21. If one thought could be the object of another thought, there would be an endless echo of thoughts of thoughts, and memory would be confused.

You can analyze an idea or an emotion and mull it over. But the actual thought cannot be the subject of another thought. Going back to the example of the mind being like a mirror, it would be like putting two mirrors together, facing each other, creating that weird effect of an endless sequence of reflections. That, Patanjali says, would fry your memory circuits.

The practical corollary is that thoughts are not real things. And they are certainly not you. You need never identify with a thought or feeling. Let them come and go.

22. The soul is unchanging but can perceive the mind when it assumes the form of what it observes.

The mirror fills up with the image of what is before it. The real you remains unchanged and eternal, but as the mirror of the mind is directed here and there, it fills up with the image in front of it, and the soul can perceive it.

23. The mind can thus be directed inward or outward onto any object.

The mirror of the mind can be used to see yourself, the soul, or anything else.

We can focus our mind on anything, so what will your focus be? And how will that affect your wellbeing?

24. The mind, with its countless subliminal impressions, operates in conjunction with the senses for a purpose beyond itself.

The mind is part of a complex machine: the body, which is occupied by the soul. This complex device serves only for the purpose of the soul. Just as a car exists for the driver and not for itself, the mind and body are there for us.

The last ten verses have presented how yoga sees consciousness and reality, and how these views contrast with those of different Buddhist groups that had influence back when Patanjali compiled his text.

These verses establish the difference between yoga metaphysics and what is known as idealism, common to many strands of Buddhism. Idealism is the philosophy that everything is just mental or mentally constructed and that there is no such thing as reality outside your mind.

Yoga presents reality in a more practical, common-sense manner than does idealism—more aligned with our experience of life.

25. When *viveka* is attained, all questions about the self come to an end.

It's natural and healthy to have questions about the self, God, and nature. That's what human life is all about. To raise and investigate questions about our existence is to make great use of this life. Where have we come from? Where are we going? To not ask such questions is a waste of the human experience.

But once perfection is attained, all questions are answered. What once seemed so complicated becomes simple. All your doubts vanish when you *experience* spiritual reality. You will have direct perception of transcendence in this path.

26. Focused on *viveka*, the mind gravitates toward *kaivalya*.

When the mind is in a state of connection and spiritual alertness, it naturally gravitates toward pure spiritual freedom, *kaivalya*.

A hungry person thinks of food. A lusty person thinks of sex. A greedy person thinks of money. And a yogi who sees the distinction between matter and spirit naturally thinks and speaks about *kaivalya*.

27. When the mind becomes distracted, other thoughts surge, according to one's previous subliminal impressions.

Until final liberation is achieved and you're really out of here, non-yogic thoughts will come in an "on-off" manner. When you're on, you're focused, in *viveka*, in loving connection. Then the mind slips and you're thinking about something mundane, in forgetfulness of God and your spiritual identity.

The more advanced you are, the more you're on. You have to work on it, making a constant effort. The more you do, the more natural it will become. Because it feels better and you perform better when you're on, you have all the incentive you need.

28. Removing these distractions removes all suffering.

As, through practice, you gradually purify your mind, you experience increasing peace and bliss. You can easily detect that thoughts born out of mundane attachment are troublesome and disturbing.

You experience directly that you're better off when you're conscious of God and your spiritual identity, seeing how everything flows naturally and how your actions and words bring about the best possible results.

29. For those in *viveka* who don't become attached even to the fruits of their wisdom, *samadhi* comes, with an abundance of *dharma*.

Viveka brings about all kinds of wonderful benefits—from peace to yogic superpowers—for living better here and now. Ultimately, though, the yogi becomes detached from all of them, as they are manifestations of the illusion of material life. In this state, he or she attains the perfection of *dharma*: full spiritual consciousness.

As you may recall, *dharma* can mean "essence." Our deepest, most real essence is our spiritual identity and connection with God. In the perfection of yoga, we experience this endless wonderful *dharma* in unlimited bliss for all eternity.

30. From this all suffering and karma ends.

This is liberation. Freedom from all karma. Freedom from all suffering. Forever.

31. At this point, all impurities are overcome and limitless knowledge arises.

There have been several sutras about the yogi's state of full knowledge, so we should take a closer examination of this to dispel any confusion.

The all-knowing state of the yogi is nothing like God's omniscience. God knows everything because He is everywhere and with everyone since forever and has perfect memory and recall.

In contrast, the yogi has, after countless lifetimes of darkness, only recently gotten his or her head out of the sand and so does not have access to all information, from all the different universes, from infinite souls, for all eternity. Clearly, it would be impossible to access, much less process, all that data.

But the yogi can understand everything in a general way. All doubts are removed. Everything he or she needs to know is known. All decisions are perfectly clear and correct.

To better understand this, we can refer to verse 15.15 of the *Bhagavad-gita*, in which Krishna explains that all knowledge, forgetfulness, and remembrance comes from Him. The yogi will thus receive all the guidance he or she *needs* from God, without interference from a clouded or distracted mind.

32. This perfect knowledge ends the involvement in the *gunas* and their endless transformations for the yogi, their purpose now fulfilled.

With perfect knowledge, the yogi becomes free of illusion, starting with the misidentification with matter and the body. No longer confused, with perfect *viveka*, the yogi lives his or her pure spiritual existence.

The yogi no longer needs the *gunas*. He or she no longer needs the virtual-reality experience of material life, since there is no more need to chase after any material situation.

A video game player can quit at any time. No longer interested in the world of the video game, the avatars, the other players, the powers, or game objectives, the player no longer has need for it.

Just like that, the yogi quits the game of *samsara* and no longer needs the *gunas* to play. He or she has now rediscovered something much more fulfilling.

33. This transformation is recognized at the end as a sequence of moments.

As you bring your mind to the here and now in intense mindfulness, you can better perceive the distinction between you and material reality. In the moment, the flow of things in the material world seems to pause, breaking its hold over us, if only for a brief instant.

Life in the material world is a sequence of such moments, and as you bring your attention to yourself, to the witness of this sequence, you experience *viveka*.

34. *Kaivalya* is when the *gunas* retreat, the soul sees that there is zero value in material existence, and the power of consciousness is situated in its pure spiritual identity.

This is the grand finale of the *Yoga Sutras*—a beautiful sutra defining perfect freedom and liberation in yoga.

Material existence serves two purposes. For countless ages, it serves the soul by providing one illusionary existence after another, according to the soul's misguided desires and merits. Then, at the end of the soul's journey through the realm of material existence, those same *gunas* help it attain freedom.

At this point, the soul understands that it has no need for the *gunas*—neither for pursuing hopeless fantasies nor for illumination. So the *gunas* retract. Or, more precisely, the yogi extracts him- or herself from them.

It's important to remember this excerpt from this sutra: "The soul sees that there is zero value in material existence." Repeat it to yourself whenever your mundane desires get the better of you. *Shunya-artha* = "zero value."

Better yet, liberation means that you get to be yourself again. Fully yourself. You re-discover your pure spiritual identity as an endless loving person in association with infinitely beautiful souls and face to face with the Supremely Lovable Lord.

Conclusion

Don't be surprised if you haven't understood a lot of this stuff. Patanjali did not compose the *Yoga Sutras* with you in mind, unless you're a 2,000-year-old mystic in the Indian wilderness.

Some parts of this book just aren't suited for you and me. We don't need tips on how to develop superpowers with advanced forms of meditation. That's like explaining to a penniless person the different options for tricking out lavish yachts. Not very useful. Likewise, you probably weren't buying into Buddhist idealism, so you didn't need dozens of sutras defeating it.

And we generally don't need books explaining difficult subjects we know nothing about in a cryptic style.

But having said that, I'm hoping you have noticed what a treasure trove of insights you can get from this book. I have tried to bring out the good stuff, and I know you can benefit from it.

I'm also hoping you don't stop here. If this is your first sojourn in the realm of yoga wisdom, there's a lot more for you. Even better than the *Yoga Sutras* is the *Bhagavad-gita*. The *Gita* is much more popular than the *Yoga Sutras* and has several advantages:

1. It's much bigger. With 701 verses—not just compacted sutras, but actual verses in meter—it presents a lot more information, and in a manner more easily understood.
2. It's target audience is you and me. It plays out like a conversation between God and Arjuna, a great warrior who starts out having the worst day of his life. Arjuna is a man of the world. He's got a job, responsibilities, family, property, and a ton of stress.
3. There isn't a single line in the *Gita* that's not applicable to us today. It's universal and timeless, loaded with profound wisdom and practical instructions.
4. By traditional estimates, it's thousands of years older than the *Yoga Sutras*. It presents itself as the original re-introduction of yoga on Earth. It's the most ancient, well-preserved, and valued text on spirituality, yoga, the soul, karma, reincarnation, and God.

There are many versions of the *Gita*. I recommend *A Comprehensive Guide to Bhagavad-gita with Literal Translation* by H.D. Goswami, my spiritual master. He wrote it with almost fifty years of deep yoga practice on top of a Ph.D. in Sanskrit and Indian Studies from

Harvard. It's brilliant, authentic, and deep, and it won't mislead you with poor translations or twisted interpretations of the original text.

I further recommend that you read my other book, *The 3T Path*. Ancient scriptures are wonderful, but it's essential to hear a modern presentation of the whole yoga path if you really want to practice it today. In *The 3T Path*, you'll find a step-by-step guide of what yoga really is and how you can apply it to your life. The information is arranged in a way that is suitable to our systematic modern way of thinking, with practical techniques, suggestions, and information from current scientific research. I get amazing feedback on a daily basis from people who, using it, are changing their lives.

Finally, though, don't just read about yoga—practice it. Make it part of your life. Give it a try, and you'll see just how powerful it is. If you're already doing *asanas* and some meditation, go deeper. Use the information in this book, the *Gita*, and other works to unlock your full potential to create a wonderful life for you and those around you.

Finished 17/12/17 at Pandavas' Paradise

About the Author

Giridhari Das, or Giri for short is a self-help and spiritual teacher, author, and speaker. He has been practicing *bhakti*-yoga, the yoga of devotion, and working with self-development for over 20 years. His mission is to present the 3T Path, a transformative process to meet and transcend the challenges of life in the 21st Century, based on the knowledge of yoga found in both ancient Sanskrit texts and the latest research in the fields of positive psychology and neuroscience. The 3T Path can be easily understood and applied as a means of self-improvement and self-realization in the world today.

Giri was born in Prague in 1969 as Gustavo Dauster, the son of a Brazilian diplomat. A few years later he and his family returned to Brazil, where he stayed until he was 9 years old. Then he moved to London where he lived for the next 8 years and studied at the American High School. Later he spent a year in the USA at Brown University and, after permanently moving back to Brazil, completed his degree in economics.

His career was just beginning when he was introduced to the *bhakti* path through a business contact. He spoke to him about Krishna consciousness, and his wife gave him a copy of the *Bhagavad-gita As It Is*. He was impressed with the knowledge found there and soon become seriously committed to the path, the daily practices and the studies.

In 1993, he met his spiritual master, Hridayananda Das Goswami Acharyadeva, and after developing a close relationship with him as his disciple, he took formal initiation in 1998, receiving from him the spiritual name, Giridhari Das.

For many years, he participated actively in ISKCON in various positions of administration and leadership in Brazil. For 10 years he was in charge of the Brazilian branch of the BBT, the publishing house of the Hare Krishna movement, and after that he served for several years as president of the governing body of ISKCON Brazil.

Today he owns and runs a Yoga Resort called Pandavas Paradise in Chapada dos Veadeiros in the highland plateaus of central Brazil. He lives there with his wife, Charana Renu Dasi (Rhiannon Dauster), and his two young sons, Bryn Govardhana and Macsen Krishna. He met Charana in Wales in 2007 while touring with his spiritual master. She has also been practicing and teaching *bhakti*-yoga since 1999.

He enjoys teaching students and guests at their yoga resort and at other spiritual centers in Brazil and around the world, and for many years he has been teaching and guiding people through email, but more recently he began to feel the need to reach out to a larger audience and in 2014 started a YouTube channel for that purpose. He currently records videos for two YouTube channels in Portuguese and one in English. He has also published four books on yoga and self-realization in Portuguese and *The 3T Path* in English.

The focus of his teaching is the 3T Path, a systematic, modern presentation of the ancient path of self-improvement and self-realization in yoga and Krishna consciousness. He developed the 3T Path after many years of dedicated study and practice, to share his experience and realizations in *bhakti*, and to address the needs and challenges of people today.

Manufactured by Amazon.ca
Acheson, AB